MY THERAPIST SAYS...

Advice You Should Probably (Not) Follow

FROM THE FOUNDERS OF
my therapist says

ROCK POINT
QUARTOKNOWS.COM
NEW YORK, NY

Inspiring | Educating | Creating | Entertaining

Brimming with creative inspiration, how-to projects, and useful information to enrich your everyday life, Quarto Knows is a favorite destination for those pursuing their interests and passions. Visit our site and dig deeper with our books into your area of interest: Quarto Creates, Quarto Cooks, Quarto Homes, Quarto Lives, Quarto Drives, Quarto Explores, Quarto Gifts, or Quarto Kids.

Text © 2020 by My Therapist Says

First published in 2020 by Rock Point, an imprint of The Quarto Group, 142 West 36th Street, 4th Floor, New York, NY 10018, USA T (212) 779-4972 F (212) 779-6058 www.QuartoKnows.com

Rock Point titles are also available at discount for retail, wholesale, promotional and bulk purchase. For details, contact the Special Sales Manager by email at specialsales@quarto.com or by mail at The Quarto Group, Attn: Special Sales Manager, 100 Cummings Center Suite, 265D, Beverly, MA 01915, USA.

10 9 8 7 6 5 4 3 2 1

ISBN: 978-1-63106-737-2

Library of Congress Control Number: 2020938588

Publisher: Rage Kindelsperger
Creative Director: Laura Drew
Managing Editor: Cara Donaldson
Senior Editor: Erin Canning
Cover and Interior Design: Amy Sly

Printed in China

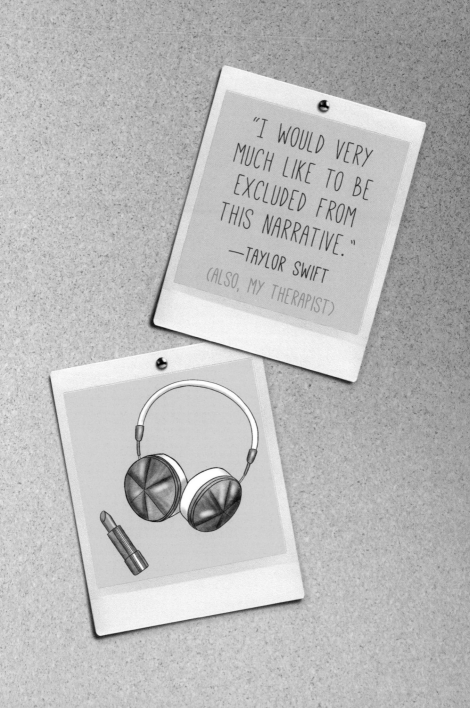

Contents

I DON'T HATE YOU BECAUSE YOU'RE A CAROL. YOU'RE A CAROL BECAUSE I HATE YOU.

Terms to Live By

Thank me later when these quick and handy terms help you describe someone/something much faster than explaining to, say, a Carol for hours why she is, in fact, a Carol.

CAROL: The annoying friend/coworker/nuisance that pesters you with her presence and infuriates you just by being her generally upbeat and keener self. Always wants to do the "right thing." Probably has a cat(s).

SUSAN: Noun and verb. Unpleasant, annoying, and delusional, the Susan is somebody who is literally awful in every way, is liked by no one, but has no clue, no matter how many open clues you give her. If you roll your eyes at this, you're probably a Susan. Uses: Susaning, Susanism. (See page 88 to learn about The Susan.)

CHAD OR BRAD: The frat-bro type of person who you love to hate, and unfortunately, can't be without. It could be anyone from the douchebag guy you keep going back to and low-key, high-key hate yourself for, or the guy who never grew out of his "Let's get fucked up!" stage. In summary, you never want to be a Chad or a Brad.

So, You Agree?
You Think I'm
Really Funny?

The music is too loud and everywhere you turn, bodies are pressed up against each other, swaying to the rhythm. Like Lindsay Lohan on top of the DJ booth in Mykonos, you're in that state of euphoria in which you feel invincible and as though any wish is within reach. It's the rare kind of confidence provided only by copious amounts of alcohol, and lighting that's too dim. That's sort of what I want every day to be like, but better. I strive, constantly, for that elusive idea of perpetual happiness. Of course, I'm not *completely* delusional, and know it's unrealistic to be living in a constant state between "responsible adult" and "low-key blackout." But, as I carry on, day by day, not necessarily learning from my mistakes, but trying my very best not to repeat them, I still chase the unattainable. The successful career. The best boyfriend. The newest clothes. The most fun group of friends.

That's the reason I wrote this magnum opus on all things to do, or better yet, not to do. My sage advice has been carefully curated through years of wrong turns, bad decisions, and half-sober therapy sessions. Most of my life, like the clichéd millennial I am, has been filled with anxiety, delusion, depression, avocado toast, euphoria, and all the unhealthy instability that comes with zero moderation. That is, until I met my therapist.

My relationship with my therapist, with its biting rapport, insatiable curiosity for life, and a familial dynamic,

has made quite an impression on people all over the globe— five million followers on Instagram and counting (my therapist has left the chat)! I began to chronicle our relationship in the form of memes on Insta, and in no time, I had legions of fans (cue crickets) telling me that they're just like me! Look, my mother would say being in my company, even figuratively, isn't a compliment, and does not even come close to anything worth bragging about, but you'll hear more about her later. Her questionable influence on me is prevalent through the fits of self-deprecation and delusional confidence gently woven within this book.

My therapist and I, however, are the true stars of this tale. We disagree on almost everything, and our road has been paved with a few obstacles here and there, including times when she tried to pass me off to colleagues; times when she conveniently "didn't see" me out in public, even though I was waving rather maniacally and watched her promptly turn around; and even times when she "lost her phone" for months to avoid the, and I quote, "headache."

People tend to enjoy this raucous dynamic in which I make a slight error, or two, or, like, six, and my therapist wonders whether I can honestly call myself a functioning human being capable of using my last two brain

S	M	T	W	T	F	S
W	R	I	T	I	N	G
M	Y					
M	A	G	N	U	M	
O	P	U	S		♡	

cells. Her words, not mine. Sure, she pleads with me to make decisions that will benefit me and not take us back eight years. Also, sure, she thought that "adopted by the Kardashians" should not be my answer when people asked me what I wanted to be when I grew up. And yes, I've been known to misread (every) situation now and again, forgoing all reason and thought, and following only my (incredibly flawed) intuition. But slowly, I am becoming the version(s?) of myself she may eventually come to publicly acknowledge, so this is all part of the learning process and journey on which we are about to embark. Together.

With my current karmic journey doing me zero favors, the time for change is now. I decided to impart the wisdom I've learned, with my therapist's impatient guidance and exasperated twitch, to all the girls, like me, who roam this world, aimless and confused as to why they constantly keep making the same mistakes over and over again, dating the same awful version of their dad, and tolerating their annoying boss's whiny nagging.

I divided this book into six chapters that cover all the bases, ranging from self-love (or, honestly, self-like, because even I can't convince others to stomach me for more than a day) and relationships, to career advice and the ever-dreaded adulting. I also included cautionary tales of things my friends have done, every now and again, to remind people that they're not alone in making colossal mistakes and seemingly ruining their reputations overnight because they decided to date a Scorpio. (Oops, have I said too much?) Oh, and yes, I've brought the ancient science that is astrology, amid all the general wisdom, to warn you of the dangers of investing time in dating a water sign, because, no, there are NOT "*so* many fish in the sea." GET OUT OF THAT SEA, ARIEL. Along with observations I've collected from nights out, and from the cubicle next to the guy who smells like sardines, I explored every avenue and left no stone unturned in my quest to guide you like your own personal Deepak Chopra, but if he had no qualifications. Quite often, during all my advice-giving, and ruminations, I even placed myself at the scene of the metaphoric crime, like a wannabe Christiane Amanpour.

I went so far as to ask my Instagram followers to submit their most burning and yearning questions, and chose, with careful deliberation, the ones that we (my bestie therapist and I) could dissect, digress, and learn from. These followers are from all over the world, varying in age, appearance, and goals, and come to think of it . . . they only have one thing in common: MTS. They want my unimpeachable advice. Okay, so maybe that's kind of a stretch, but they want the combined intellect and experience of my therapist, along with the take-charge, innovative approach of moi.

Throughout, my therapist interjects and intervenes in areas she feels necessary (aka in areas she feels I've advised you so horribly that it should be illegal that I have a platform to engage with the masses).

As in vogue as it currently is to wreak havoc, I hope, with the tools provided in this book, you can do so with your sanity, and well-being, intact, and go on to conquer the world. The journey to finding your inner Beyoncé starts now.

I Guess You're My Boyfriend?

(The Dating, the Relationships & the Breakups)

ME @ MYSELF: CAN YOU NOT?!

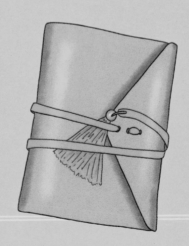

The Chase
(and the Girls Who Like It)

The story goes as follows: Girl meets boy, they fall in love, everything seems to be going great, then, just as suddenly, it's not. Girl waits, and waits, passing it off as an instance here, a moment there. She overthinks and overanalyzes every date they've had, trying to pinpoint the moment it all changed. But, what she doesn't know is that while she was falling in love, boy was already moving on to the next conquest.

A majority of the questions people have asked over the years have been centered around love—relationships, cheating, dates, fuckboys, etc. As we all know, nothing is more addictive than an all-consuming, bad-for-you relationship in which you are left with nothing but a dependency on alcohol (or chocolate; tacos; shopping; insert anything, really), a new Netflix show, and remnants of a broken heart. My natural advice to almost every single one of these questions is "no" and "dump him," I realized it would be callous to generalize every male into one category, not to mention incredibly unfair.

However, there is one exception and you can generalize this type of person very easily without feeling any sort of guilt: The Fuckboy.

The F*ckboy

- ☐ May have a man bun

- ☐ Very into fitness and his general appearance

- ☐ Texts a million girls to see "what's up" only to pick the best "option"

- ☐ Definitely has some trauma

- ☐ Thinks feminism is for "angry women"

- ☐ Will tell you he's not "ready" for a relationship but cares for you

THINK: Leonardo DiCaprio, 1 OAK

We all know this person. We've all, at one point or another, been in love with a variation of this person, only to realize, no, we *don't* hate ourselves. And I'm not saying that this term is reserved exclusively for men; there are plenty of women out there who also engage in this type of behavior, constantly in pursuit of something better, only to end up feeling rather empty inside. Quite often, it's not even malicious; it's habitual—they don't know any other way to survive. They go to clubs and bars, thriving at night, in search of where the grass might be greener, never truly satisfied with what they have. Any form of attachment is terrifying, and the thought of being "caught" in the trappings of a relationship is disconcerting because life should "always be fun." No, John Mayer, this isn't a personal attack on you.

The F*ckboy Checklist

❑ Y ❑ N Does he use words like "vibe," "mood," "vibrations," "synergy," "wanderlust," and "baddie" sincerely?

❑ Y ❑ N Does he ask you to follow him on social media before asking for your number or your name?

❑ Y ❑ N Does he say things like, "I don't need an education. I've learned more in the school of hard knocks, the school of life."

❑ Y ❑ N Does he ask you what your zodiac sign is?

❑ Y ❑ N Does he bite his lip and slightly squint his eyes as though staring into the sun when posing for a photo?

❑ Y ❑ N Does he refer to his outfit as a "fit"?

❑ Y ❑ N Does he say Leonardo DiCaprio deserved his Oscar years before he won one and that he is "the greatest artist and humanitarian of our generation"?

❑ Y ❑ N Does he notice the brands you're wearing, piece by piece, and say, "Swag," while nodding his head?

❑ Y ❑ N Does his bio on Instagram have airport abbreviations to describe cities he's lived in?

❑ Y ❑ N Does he have more than two cities listed in his bio?

☐ Y ☐ N Is Off-White his favorite brand?

☐ Y ☐ N Does he own a fanny pack/bucket hat that may or may not say "Balenciaga"?

☐ Y ☐ N Both?

☐ Y ☐ N Does he go to Cipriani every weekend, claiming that it's his "second home"?

☐ Y ☐ N Does he say that he "usually doesn't go out during the week," while being out every night?

☐ Y ☐ N Does he follow the Victoria's Secret Angels roster on Instagram and comment under their photos as though they're friends?

☐ Y ☐ N Does he like Drake more than his family?

☐ Y ☐ N Does he make plans by texting "wyd"?

Honestly, if you've checked YES for even one of these, you need to run. Or evaluate yourself and your decisions, and why you feel that it's "not that bad" that he considers 1 OAK a "fun place."

Tip: For a fun drinking game, take a shot each time one of these applies to whom you're dating or your dating history. If you're tipsy by the time you've gone through the list, it's time to end it.

I like my men

how I like my alcohol—

with a chase.

This guy will lead you on, trying you on for size, seeing whether you could fit his ideal, unrealistic girlfriend mold—a mythical dream that simply does not exist. He does what most of us do: keeps searching. But time and time again, his searches prove to be failures, because no matter how far and wide he may search, he'll end up hollow and alone, thinking everything was his choice, that he still retains control, and that he just hasn't found that one quality he was looking for in a person yet.

Dear God, I think I just saw a subtle nod of approval from my therapist, meaning she, omg, agrees with me.

Or she has a twitch.

The One Who Doesn't Know What He Wants
(but Makes You Think He Wants You)

This is the worst kind of guy to date, because he will get you used to him, act like a boyfriend, and then realize something about you just isn't right. So, like the confused coward he is, he can't quite break things off with you, but slowly, he will retreat as surely as he came. Like ghosting, but slightly nobler. He's dangerous because he truly doesn't believe what he's doing is bad.

My therapist probably feels unequivocal rage, and this is one point we both agree on. Okay, so the rage is mine, but she agrees.

 My Therapist Says it's hard to immediately identify this person because anyone, at any point, can suddenly change their mind and become this version of themselves. It's infuriating, but she also says it's technically not always intentional. If you do happen to encounter this type of person, and to your best knowledge, you know that this behavior isn't foreign to him, extricate yourself from the situation. Leave his life as gracefully as you came. But I don't think she means chug half a bottle of tequila while grinding to Drake, because that's sort of how we met.

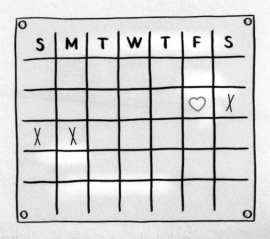

IF PURPOSELY WAITING
TO RESPOND TO A GUY'S
MESSAGES FOR THREE DAYS
IS WRONG, I DON'T WANT
TO BE RIGHT.

Now, *my* advice would be to start playing the weirdest fucking games with him. Don't respond to his messages for three days, and then hit him up with a casual "'sup?" when the time is right. Flirt with other guys in front of him, so he knows what a catch he has, and never forget to master the art of acting like you just don't care. About anything. What he says, what he does, his opinion—it's all kind of *meh*. And when HE asks you what's wrong, act completely confused and cavalier, because you're just. That. Chill.

My therapist does not condone, endorse, or in any way approve of anything I wrote in the last paragraph.

Um, okay, like I thought that she had that kind of thrill for life in her?

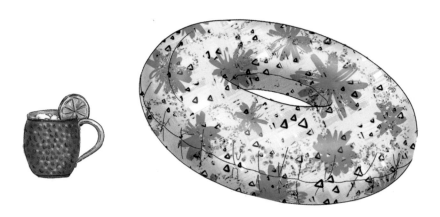

Why Do I Keep Dating the Human Embodiment of Syphilis?

Dear MTS,

I'm so single. Like, so single that I'm confused because I always have so many dates, but they all end up being the same, and I don't know if it's a case of me attracting the wrong guys, or me pursuing the wrong ones. Help!

—Kaitlynn

This definitely touched a nerve with me, as I notoriously pursue the same real-life version of a Voldemort-type guy, consistently. Like, it would be funny, if I wasn't so incredibly traumatized and disturbed, all while continuing to inflict the same trauma on myself, time and time again. Kaitlynn, like myself, needs a harsh and imminent reality check.

If something isn't working out, don't keep trying and trying again because all those pathetic Pinterest quotes (probably written by a Susan) tell you to. Um, there's probably a reason it literally NEVER works out.

My friend Veronica, and I seriously mean friend (this isn't a pseudonym for me and I'm too pathetic to admit it), is one of us in the dysfunctional-daters club. Her preferred aphrodisiac is a guy who is so openly unavailable, you'd have to actually hate yourself to willingly apply for the job of removing the douche from this person.

My preferred method is to treat men who I actually might have a successful future with, poorly, and focus on the men who I would classify as "moments," telling my friends trying to knock any sense into me to "fuck off," because I'm having a "MOMENT." This is a real thing I truly despise about myself, but any guy who seems like a "moment," hit me up! (*see also:* another reason I'm in therapy)

Qualities of a "Moment" Checklist

☐ Narcissist

☐ Asshole

☐ Probably hot (not always necessary tho ☹)

☐ Liar

☐ Manipulative

☐ Smart (which is usually how they're so manipulative)

☐ Intuitive (this, again, aids them in their quest of ruining you)

☐ Damaged

THE ONLY "MOMENTS" I SHOULD BE HAVING ARE IN THERAPY.

The Antidote

Kaitlynns of the world, the time is now for us to look in the mirror and figure out what it is we don't like about ourselves, to keep putting ourselves through the cruelty and indecency of dating the scum of the Earth. What we must do is observe all the traits we are innately drawn to, quash them within ourselves, and against all odds, pursue the people who are actually interested in us. I know. *Revolutionary.* Some girls will say that it's the assholes pursuing them and not the other way around, and frankly, I don't fucking care. Have a semblance of respect and know your worth to not allow yourself to be subjected to that kind of treatment. Not to sound like an after-school special, but you deserve more than a Ryan Howard.

My therapist is also saying something along these lines, but sans the profanity.

Another harrowing reality is what the type of guy we attract says about us. Are we really so unpleasant/karmically fucked that we are plagued with this genetic error over and over again? Like, why are we the chosen ones taking on this task and not, say, the girls who match their birthdays with the guys they're dating to see if they're astrologically compatible? If the Libra with a Gemini moon isn't punished, then why do *I* have to suffer? (*see also:* the entire astrology chapter I wrote dedicated to this, so who am I to talk)

I suppose the moral here is to love yourself, which will hopefully steer you away from the awful men who clearly don't love you. It's not even self-preservation at this point. It's common sense.

My therapist is quite proud of me for coming to this realization . . . five years too late.

Avoid, Avoid, Avoid

You've been warned about The Fuckboy (see page 17), but here are the other types of men you should steer clear of at ALL costs. We've all watched rom-coms in which, against all odds, including being in a relationship and unavailable in every way possible, the lead characters end up together, only to live happily ever after (for all we know, after the end credits, they could've gotten divorced). These men are the ones who will, unbeknownst to them, destroy you in every capacity and date your best friend. If you're anything like me, take notes and scour every bar for them, only to replay the monthly cycle of heartbreak *(but, also, pleeeeease don't)*.

The Frat Bro

☐ Is forever immature

☐ Thinks winning his fantasy league is a sport

☐ Probably reports back to his friends, regularly, discussing you

☐ Is always on the lookout

☐ Is looking for "fun"

☐ Is a devotee of hip-hop or deep house

☐ Uses abbreviations without any irony

☐ Thinks all feminists are lesbians

☐ ALWAYS thinks he can do better

☐ Loves Vegas

THINK: Marcus in *Something Borrowed*, Dean Sampson in *She's All That*, Stifler in *American Pie*, Leonardo DiCaprio in life

The Finance Brah (or The Guy Who Watched *The Wolf of Wall Street* Too Many Times)

- ❑ Idolizes Leonardo DiCaprio

- ❑ Treats women THE worst

- ❑ Has apparent daddy and/or mommy issues. Bonus if both!

- ❑ Has awful social skills

- ❑ Not to be confused with the Frat Bro, because he's actually educated (but very close)

- ❑ His longest relationship was probably two months (and he's impressed he lasted that long)

- ❑ Thinks everything is a deal

- ❑ Loves to discuss himself, his accomplishments, his adversaries, and his perseverance

- ❑ Will argue with you about probably everything just to show off

- ❑ Will consider you ungrateful for not noticing his nonexistent, small gestures

- ❑ ALSO Loves Vegas, Mykonos, and Ibiza, like, loooooves

THINK: Chuck Bass in *Gossip Girl*, Mr. Big in *Sex and the City*, Elton in *Clueless*

My bestie said I
shouldn't date him,
so I probably will.

"The Nice Guy" (Not to Be Confused with The Nice Guy)

- ❑ Shows conditional niceness

- ❑ Is fake/a LIAR

- ❑ Will eventually grow to hate you because you "led him on" (so, also delusional, unless you actually did lead him on)

- ❑ Says he's a feminist but is reverting women back 100 years

- ❑ Says he "just gets along better with women"

- ❑ Likes, and comments on, all your photos, but will block you if you don't respond

- ❑ Gets to know all of your female friends, only so he can text them after you reject him

- ❑ Incessantly sends you passive-aggressive memes

- ❑ Signs every online petition but won't be able to explain to you what it is he's signing

- ❑ Constantly tells you about his meditations/why YOU would benefit from meditation

- ❑ Quotes Marcus Aurelius constantly

- ❑ You probably met him while you were dating someone else

- ❏ There's very little evidence of him having actual guy friends

- ❏ Probably owns more than one beanie

- ❏ Spends way too much time in boutique coffee shops, working on his "script"

- ❏ Says he's the best Instagram "photographer" (he just has an artist's eye; not to be confused with The (F)Artist)

- ❏ Uses healing crystals

- ❏ Asks if you want to work out together/go hiking

- ❏ Magically appears shirtless at random times of the day, just wanting to "talk, babe"

- ❏ Calls you "darling," "babe," or "sweetheart" without irony

- ❏ Manages to make every story about how he's overcome many a hurdle

- ❏ Is probably writing his own male version of this advice book

THINK: Elton in *Clueless* (*see also:* The Finance Brah), Dan Humphrey in *Gossip Girl*, Joe Goldberg in *You* (literally, it looks like you should just steer clear of Penn Badgley)

The (F)Artist

- Thinks everything is inspiration

- Will always put you second to his "art"

- Thinks he's Andy Warhol

- Has probably never studied art

- Accessorizes better than you do

- Most likely has a broken infinity tattoo because "nothing lasts forever"

- Is always "working" (it's a mystery to everyone, including him, on what)

- Rarely showers (honestly, why are you attracted to this?)

- Has "muses" who change. And often.

- Is the worst kind of hipster

- If you want to piss him off, bring him a Starbies while he's "working"

THINK: Johnny Depp in life, Todd Cleary in *Wedding Crashers*, James Franco in almost every movie, Marilyn Manson in life

 My Therapist Says if a man possesses three or more of the qualities I mentioned in this section, it's unlikely he's ready for, or capable of, a serious relationship, and trying will only leave you hurt and confused, like you did something wrong.

So, You've Tricked Someone into Dating You?

Oh, look! You're a few dates deep and he hasn't blocked your number or accused you of stalking him during one of those casual drive-bys you're so fond of. He's the first person you send a particularly good meme to, and the one you tag in food accounts. Basically, you're in a relationship, but these days, putting a label on things is so dated, and yet so unequivocally necessary, because EVERYTHING is so unclear. We all want our existence somewhat acknowledged by our partner, whether it's through a sly Insta pic or an outright proclamation of devotion people are so fond of these days in the form of some spectacularly bad poetry, under a photo of the two of you gazing longingly into the distance in Malibu made to look like Cabo.

The Clinger

This is all great and lovely, and romance is not dead, but beware: do not become the Clinger. You either know the Clinger, you have a Clinger, or you are the Clinger. This is very much not a myth; it is a terrifying reality. If your presence isn't exciting the guy, and most reactions are a bit "meh," you're def clinging on and he's over it.

This brings me to my absolute favorite point in any and every relationship: you can never, under any circumstances, gun to your head, stop playing games!

WHEN HE THINKS YOU'RE CLINGY BUT HE'S ONLY SEEN STAGE 5. :))))

At Least Pretend to Be Cool

The thing about being in a relationship is that when it's really great, you start to mess things up. You question things, you overanalyze, you become suspicious; you start looking for flaws, because the thought of something truly being as good as it seems is terrifying. You're vulnerable, and you're attached, and now, you've got something to lose.

My Therapist Says that the fear of losing something shouldn't keep you from playing the game, whatever blah, blah—this was in a Hilary Duff movie. Boring. But why are we so reckless and destructive when we don't care?

And it's when we don't care that things start working toward our benefit, instead of all those laborious hours of caring falling straight into our detriment. If you go on without a care in the world, you start to loosen up and have fun, but the second you're with a guy you see a future with, out goes your sanity, and in comes Gloria Cleary.

Not caring seems like a waste of time, and not worth the effort, so I never pursue people who I know will elicit zero reactions from me. The trick, however, is to utilize that blasé, carefree attitude with men you *do* care about, so you approach that relationship from a place of freedom, without limitations. When you care too much, you add rules—things to

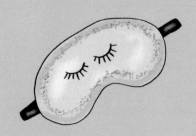

I have 99 problems

and caring too much

is literally all of them.

avoid, things not to say, things you hope they don't say, checking off lists—all in the pursuit that this just might be the one. But throughout all this, you're waiting, without fail, for them to fail. Even though we tell ourselves we hope "this time it's different," we never truly brace ourselves for it, do we? All these restrictions and rules drive us to madness, and that madness invites a lot of unwanted baggage into a relationship, weighing it down before it even has a chance to flourish.

So, be selfish and be excited when approaching your dating life, but don't do it from a place of "this is it." Make room for many moments that could be "it," so you can enjoy the full experience of something potentially exciting. Like that *Eat Pray Love* movie, be chill. If you're unable to extricate the crazy from the lady, then ride that roller coaster to your advantage, and keep the guy on his toes. I've been doing this for years and I can honestly say that it's never been dull. Successful? Mmm, questionable.

The Never-Ending Games

Games are integral to the livelihood of your relationship . . . and to everything you are. You think that sounds dramatic? No. Dramatic is what you're going to want to do to yourself when he starts cheating on you/breaks up with you/insert any way to leave you for a girl who's so cleverly stringing him along for the ride of his life in a van full of guys she's not 100 percent into but not yet ready to let go of. THAT is the truth. Some of you will now preach that your relationship is different, and built on a solid foundation of love, values, and virtues, and literally, I will be here, saying, "I told you so," in the pettiest way possible, but with a heavy heart, because nobody ever listens to this. Speaking from experience here (the experience of myself and, like, ten good friends), this is not a drill.

People hear the words "playing games" and automatically assume it's this torturous, arduous exercise of testing your partner's limits and commitment. God, no! Do I seem like a sadistic sociopath hell-bent on ending your relationship before it even begins? I'm referring to the delicate art of not quite giving a fuck and caring too much. This is for your benefit more than anything. Men, like literally everything in your life, for the most part, are unreliable. They're good when they're great, but as time passes, so does the (hoping you had this) fiery passion that drew you to this person in the first place. Again, this isn't always the case, but it's better to assume the worst and be prepared for it.

That's human nature, and I think every person can attest to having withdrawn after a period of time has lapsed. THIS IS WHY GAMES WERE INVENTED: to keep the interest alive and well, and the mystery so ridiculously confusing, that half the time, even you don't know how it'll

MAYBE SHE'S BORN WITH IT, MAYBE SHE'S PLAYING GAMES.

end. My best friend, Ashley, plays games so well that 99 percent of her exes still can't get over her because of the Rubik's Cube that is her brain. We don't talk about the 1 percent.

My therapist refuses to encourage acting unreasonable for the sole reason of keeping the mystique alive, believing that to be a terrible manipulation.

It is now my turn to roll my eyes at her, and quite obnoxiously, may I add.

I'm not saying to peace out for three days—no phone call or explanation—and come back being like, "What's new?" I mean, in the simplest way, always keep just a little bit of mystery in the relationship—you don't have to know every single thing he does and who he does it with, and vice versa. It's what you don't say that counts. Moving on.

The Game Playing Doctrine

This playing-hard-to-get manifesto is dedicated to every girl (or boy) who has had to wait more than the obligatory 5 seconds for a text back. As if.

- When he asks you what you're up to, don't give more than a one- or two-line response. Sound busy.

- Take up an interest without him, so you have something separate from each other to then discuss and bring you closer together.

- Conveniently forget to charge your phone when going out for drinks with friends. (just kidding, kind of ;))

- Keep a healthy social life that doesn't revolve around him. Even in the honeymoon phase, try to keep it balanced.

- Have an identity outside of being a couple, so your every other sentence doesn't start with "we" and "us."

The Fam
(His and, Ugh, Yours)

You may think devoting a whole section to this topic is excessive, but so many relationships are reliant on how the family sees you and him. Your future depends on these precious, fragile moments that could take you from girlfriend to straight down that aisle. One too many accessories, a chipped manicure, a bad hair day, or a nasty hangover, and you can kiss the family jewels goodbye. All of them. (Yes, I mean both metaphoric and physical.)

Meeting His Family

If he's particularly close to his family (and that's a good thing; you don't need more issues to be dealing with), you want to impress them because it will mean a lot to him. Like, if his brother hates you, he's going to be constantly there, mumbling unflattering things, eventually driving him to question why he's dating you in the first place. Even worse is if his brother *does* like you, like too much, and things get uncomfortable. This is why you must always try incredibly hard to make the family love and respect you, but in a *familial* way. I cannot stress the importance of this enough.

Quite often, a man's approach to his relationships is to emulate what he witnessed growing up. This can sound both comforting and terrifying. If you've had the misfortune of accidentally sticking around through a whole

ME? FAKE? NEVERRRR. *LOGS OUT OF FINSTA*

episode of *Criminal Minds*, you know that that kind of statement often doesn't end well. Hoping and praying that he comes from a relatively normal family, you will summon all the strength you have within you, and Blake Lively your way through the whole ordeal. I don't care if you have to pretend to love baking and whip up (order) a pavlova so good it would make Gordon Ramsay proud.

No matter the family dynamic, you need to act sweet, cultured, well mannered, and interesting. These are the people who will either encourage or heavily discourage your boyfriend to put a ring on it, or whatever your goal is.

His Parent(s)

Mothers tend to be the keys that unlock every familial Pandora's box and the guardians of approval. With their support, you can conquer any family member, be they an overly opinionated uncle or a questionable niece. She'll prepare you, grooming you as her heir, with very little patience and deliberation—like a pageant mom. If she *doesn't* like you, but you still manage to somehow marry into the family, get ready for the most challenging years of your life, until she finally ages out and relents, too tired for her fight. Only old age can disarm that vulture. Here's how to make a great first impression:

Start by complimenting the mother on literally anything you can think of, but do so sincerely, so she doesn't accuse you of being a fake bitch. I mean, you are, but she doesn't have to know that. There's no coming back after being called fake. I'm sure even my therapist will agree with that. Once you've adequately complimented her home, her appearance, and her incredible son . . .

The How to Wow
the Parents Checklist

Compliments

- ☐ The house
- ☐ The meal
- ☐ The outfits
- ☐ The dynamic

Questions

- ☐ Ask about their youth
- ☐ Ask for advice
- ☐ Come up with a pressing dilemma that you just need their opinion on

Stories (Prepare a sad and happy story to show that you are nonthreatening and kindhearted)

- ☐ Sad story
- ☐ Happy story

Move on to asking her questions, literally anything you can think of. Ask her for advice, so she knows you're deferring to her knowledge and wisdom, thereby acknowledging your place in the familial food chain. Trust me, mothers notice these things, and they care.

My therapist is sighing loudly every couple of minutes, so I think it's safe to assume she's unhappy with this.

If his parents are divorced, then do everything mentioned, and take an even deeper interest in her life/youth/hobbies. If she's single, she's going to want to talk, and probably about herself.

Do not, under any circumstance, reveal a power imbalance between you and your boyfriend, making her hate you for having such an effect on her son that he can't say no to you. This is probably the one place where not always winning may actually get you the W.

Dads, on the other hand, are usually pretty laid-back, unless they accuse you of secretly trying to get pregnant, which is actually not that uncommon at all. They won't say it to your face, but they will tell their son to proceed with caution. For the most part, you'll probably have to listen and nod to his stories, adding the appropriate "really!" or "no way, that's incredible!" Even if he is discussing lawn bowling, I want enthusiasm, ladies!

No matter how hard you try to please, and how genuinely kind you are, if the parents don't like you from the first impression, it's almost always going to stay that way. You know all those movies in which the family finds out, *eventually*, that the girl their son is dating has been this great anomaly all along, whom he is lucky to have found, and apologize for their severe judgment? Unrealistic. Doesn't exist.

His Sibling(s)

Sometimes, the only thing worse than encountering strict parents is being introduced to the ready-to-hate-you sister. His sister cares for him, and she believes that every girl is out to get him for the wrong reasons.

I mean, *literally* nobody in his family will acknowledge how lucky this ogre is to have you. Instead of being offended, and rightfully so, try to understand how you would react if you had a brother and he brought a girl home. Sure, you'd like to say you would be the picture of serenity and calm, giving the girl the benefit of the doubt, but realistically, that's not your first instinct. We are often more protective of others than we are of ourselves. Remember *Monster-in-Law*? Yeah, we would ALL be Jane Fonda.

To appease a sister, just act as unassuming as possible, and try to find a common language. Whether it's liking the same books, movies, fashion, political icon, or literally anything, try to find a common interest and proceed from there. If you find that she prefers, like, Slipknot or something particularly out of your realm, probably refrain from saying you think it's unfair that Britney hasn't won a Grammy for Best Album. When you have absolutely nothing in common, just pretend to like the thing you can most easily fake.

Example: If she's a fan of Hillary Clinton, be like, "Oh my God, I know. Isn't Monica just *the* worst?" Thank me later.

Did we just become best friends?!

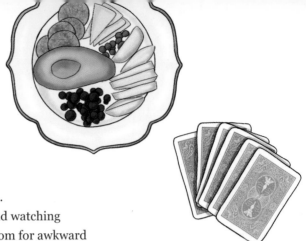

If he happens to have
a brother, just be nice
and pretend to like sports.
It almost always helps, and watching
TV doesn't leave much room for awkward
conversation and pestering questions.

Unless he has really annoying younger siblings, you should be able to slide through this unscathed. But if he does have annoying younger siblings, just pop an Advil and start playing games with them. Swallow that competitive spirit and let them win, because they'll probably tire of the game faster if they keep winning and realize you're not good at games, which will cause them to leave you alone entirely, parting on good terms.

His Misc. Family Member(s)

Now, should you encounter an overbearing grandma who instantly despises you for not knowing how to cook or a distant relative who is awful by every definition of the word, then just try to escape into the safe distance of your boyfriend and orbit there until it's time to leave. Say as little as possible without looking like a docile mute.

Tip: Smile in that magnanimous way that Angelina Jolie's face seems to be permanently frozen in and you'll be good to go, I think.

**DOES THIS BLOUSE
HIDE THE FACT THAT
I CAN THROW BACK
WHISKEY SANS
CHASER?**

Pamela Anderson Would Never!

I think it goes without saying that wearing anything overly revealing, or literally anything a Kardashian would don, is to be avoided. Now, don't start attacking me for telling women what to wear, as they've fought for years to oppose this exact thing. I'm not telling you to do this to please or to enforce a certain dress code, but out of respect for your boyfriend and his family. It will not kill you to let your cleavage feel fabric for a change instead of fresh air.

How you dress around them will be half the battle because we, as humans, first judge on what we see, and only then, after that appeases us, do we begin to listen. *Woah.* That almost sounded enlightened. No matter how intelligent or hilarious you are, nobody will listen if you're wearing something controversial. Again, this is all based on a personal preference. If you prefer to be polarizing and start a conversation, then by all means, do you. Introduce a little spontaneity into the family dynamic.

 My Therapist Says that you should be the best version of yourself, and be kind, so they get to know the true person their son is bringing home. Honesty and good character are always the way to go.

Um, if her advice is going out to any of *my* girlfriends, I think she and I can both agree that being themselves is something they should never do.

Meeting Your Family

Now, on to the truly heinous part: *your* family. If you happen to come from a perfectly normal, loving household in which everyone respects each other and casual, character-building verbal abuse is nonexistent, then you have a chance at getting through this unscathed. But, if like the majority of MTS's readers, you come from dysfunction personified, then you can start taking notes while simultaneously setting up an online-dating profile and looking for a new boyfriend.

You know how in military school they prepare students with strict time lines, rigid training, and an authoritarian mindset, only to release them into the wild world where they are thereby able to withstand the changing of any tides? That is exactly what readying your boyfriend to meet your parents is like. Or it should be.

My therapist is frowning so deeply she's starting to resemble Jafar. She definitely does not condone ingraining this negativity and hostility before a first meeting.

Um, and she, once again, is WRONG. It's all fun and games until you end up single, in your childhood bedroom, blaming your mom for the millionth time. Preparation is everything.

house RULES

- COMPLIMENT
- BE AGREEABLE
- LAUGH AT ALL
  BAD JOKES
- LIE
- MAKE IT OUT OF
  THERE ALIVE!

Your Parent(s)

My mother's favorite pastime is chronicling all of my many mistakes, sprinkling in every flaw, and topping it off by regaling everyone with tales of how superior she was to me when she was my age—moments she likes to call "character builders." This is when people are over, so she's well behaved. When reading this, if you're reminded of similar traits your mother has, then abort mission. Do not, under any circumstances, introduce him to her. Unless you secretly hate your boyfriend or something???

If he's insistent (ugh), and you somehow manage to bribe your mother into behaving like the maternal figure she once saw in a movie, then you need to play this incredibly safe. Never is he to be left alone with her for more than one-minute intervals, because two minutes will lead to severe consequences, and anything less than a minute might seem impolite!

 My Therapist Says I'm exaggerating the magnitude of the situation, but she did mention I specify that I'm exaggerating the harshness of your mothers, not my own. In regard to mine, we tend to be on the same page.

Should your mother go off script at any point throughout the meeting, escape quickly. That is usually the beginning of the end.

Arm your boyfriend with flowers, wine, and anything else it will take to subdue and impress the vulture hiding within her fortress of keen intuition and lack of facial expressions. When he's giving compliments, make sure to instruct him to keep his voice even and strong, so she doesn't detect any weakness and jump at her chance.

This may sound ridiculous to you, approaching a mother with the clinical precision reserved for doctors and scientists, but you underestimate the ferocity of a bored and/or triggered housewife/mother. When you've thoroughly pacified her and her insatiable curiosity with the man, who, against all odds, managed to be attracted to her walking liability of a daughter, you move on to dear old dad.

Your dad, seeing his girl all grown up with another man in her life, might actually make this even harder than mom, unless he's like my father, whose only wish is to finally be rid of the spinster-in-training.

If your father is somewhat protective and kind of scary, make sure your boyfriend stands his ground with confidence and humor, so your father has no reason to mentally torture him. For the most part, if you still show allegiance to your father over your boyfriend, he will be satisfied and move on. But if he's like my father, he might begin to analyze, and empathize with, the man who is dealing with his constant inconvenience (me). Reading this, you're piecing together why therapy was a must in the first place, *non*?

Your Sibling(s)

Look, we know girls are cruel. They're clever, cunning, and cutting when they want to be, and your sisters? When meeting your boyfriend? They'll want to be. They'll want to mentally assess every part of this foreign species who has been able to tolerate their sister long enough to fall in love with her and (possibly) stick it out for the long haul, which, to them, seems unfathomable and unappealing. Therefore, there must be something wrong with him. Wait, was I just describing my sisters?

Some of you, I'm hoping, are blessed with sisters who will refrain from somehow flawlessly reciting every humiliating moment in your life yet fail to remember what they had for breakfast. Maybe they'll even be charitable enough to make you sound somewhat desirable and funny—an Aphrodite by his side. If you happen to amass a fortune big enough to buy your sisters off by the time this introduction happens, bravo.

Brothers are tricky, because, like your father, they will feel a need to be protective of you. At first, they might be outright unpleasant and cold, but often, they will actually befriend your boyfriend. Just make sure

your boyfriend sounds really cool by prepping him beforehand with facts and stats about your brother's favorite team/game/anything that will induce bonding.

Also, brothers can be somewhat unpredictable, so definitely have a long talk with yours before the meeting, as he could be the black sheep coming to ruin your happily ever after.

Your Misc. Family Member(s)

I have too many rogue family members whom I can, in all honesty, never leave alone with my boyfriend, for fear they will absolutely ruin my chance at happiness. Whether intentional or not, these members are what I call basement members of the family. I love them, but until absolutely necessary, they will be kept in the basement until further notice.

When They Don't Get Along

What if after all the careful planning your family still ends up hating your boyfriend? Well, you have two choices, naturally: you can rebel and date him anyway, angering and ostracizing your family further, or you can break up with him.

This is where it becomes tricky. If they give you solid reasons for their lack of approval, with facts, receipts, and examples, then you have to consider why you're with this person.

Example: Are you just pleasantly ignoring the glaring flaws in favor of arm candy?

If the case is that he's not quite meeting the standards and hopes your family had for you, you have to seriously give it some thought: Is it worth alienating yourself from your family for somebody you're not quite sure you're going to end up with? Always keep a rational head, as these are the moments when your sanity will be tested. If your family truly makes good points, you will need to make a fair and sound decision, and proceed with caution.

My Therapist Says I've taken the whole introduction into a new level of theatrics and that it can also be fun, and exciting. Oh, like the fun and exciting times James Franco's character had in *127 Hours*? She advises to treat everyone in the scenario with respect, and that your boyfriend should do the same. Your family, if they truly care about you, will approach the situation with open hearts and minds, and hopefully, this could turn into something great. Be patient with everyone, as every family member will deal with your having a partner differently, as you mean something different to each of them. Your father might see it as losing a daughter, but try to make him see he's gaining a new friend. Be as patient and understanding as you can.

Look, I don't know what she's on right now, but that's almost never the case, so if possible, write a short play and have your family remember their lines when you bring over the boyfriend. Write a separate play for your boyfriend.

My therapist has insisted I clarify that she has never taken anything and that I should refrain from implying things in published print.

Ugh, Do I Have To?

Having tricked a guy into loving (liking?) you, you now find yourself in a serious relationship. Maybe he even met your family, and against all odds, still wants to hang around. You two decide that, in the natural progression of things, taking the next step is essential. You move in together. *I know.* Breathe. He will now have access to your leg-shaving schedule, your weird tics and annoyances, and your love of poorly made reality TV. You now have to wake up looking somewhat human, as opposed to the human-resembling thing you typically look like when home alone (unless you're one of those people who actually takes time to look presentable at home? Can't relate). Nothing will ever be the same.

Dear MTS,

I'm having a bit of a panic attack, as I'm moving in with my boyfriend in three days. I love him and I want to spend time with him, but in such close proximity?! And all the time?! I think I'm having a panic attack.

—Maria

Maria, you're not on your own. We've all felt the tremors of love turning into something more serious and concrete, sending fear through our bodies and chills down our spines. To adequately get through this tumultuous time, we need to spread this out into subsections. Yes, it's exciting to be uniting with someone you love, but it is integral to do so prepared. Dating someone and not seeing them every now and again is fine and well because they don't have access to you 24/7, but living with someone is a whole different ballgame, because there is now little in the way of privacy.

Dirty Little Secret (or Keeping the Love Alive)

Now that you and your significant other are going to be attached at the hip, almost literally, you'll have to find new and innovative ways to keep him on his toes. And, of course, vice versa. Living together is how you test your compatibility as a mature, adult couple, readying yourselves for the next steps adulthood has to offer. Whether that is a family, marriage, whatever, that's up to you, but this is definitely an important step.

The trick is getting along and enjoying each other without becoming monotonous and boring, and taking each other for granted, eventually leading to looking elsewhere and breaking up. I don't mean to be the bearer of bad news, but that's kind of a possibility, and you have to be made aware of it so it's a mistake you don't commit.

Keep yourself busy, as you would if you were living alone. You don't need to do *everything* together. Go out for little errands, make some time for yourself, and spend some time apart, so you miss each other all over again while having an identity of your own. Just because you now live together, you are not required to become one person, sharing the same interests and routine. Doing things together every now and again is great, and it'll make for a great date night, but have a life of your own, too.

If you don't love me at my hair hasn't been brushed in a week, you can't have me at my three-hour makeup tutorial.

Having something to yourself is good for a few reasons: it gives you more to talk about at the end of the day, it gives you time to cultivate yourself, and it gives you your own perspective. Being ensconced in a bubble of togetherness can lead to a biased view of things, so extricating yourself from that and changing up the scenery will be conducive to a healthy relationship.

My therapist is somewhat shocked at the wisdom I'm throwing your way, as she didn't expect this level of maturity from me.

If You're Really Messy

If you are naturally a disgusting slob, like my friend Megan, you should definitely hide the harsher aspects of that. I'm not saying change yourself to appease a man, but just don't be so gross where even a guy would be shocked. There's messy, with not picking up an article of clothing here or there, or leaving some dishes in the sink to be taken care of later, and there's Megan-messy, where the floor of the bedroom becomes as undetectable as her morals. Just try to keep it relatively clean so he doesn't start to question your other habits . . .

If You're OCD

At the opposite of really messy, you could be Monica from *Friends*, embarrassingly needing everything to be a certain way to the point where people don't want to live with you anymore. This, of course, is often out of your control and can be considered an illness, but as somebody who has battled OCD, you can conquer this with some force.

Being a neat freak is usually seen as a good thing, but just try not to take it overboard, where people feel afraid of doing anything around your apartment, in fear they might spill something. This fear will translate to your boyfriend, as he realizes he's living with a dictator. Try to be as flexible as you can in areas where maybe being obsessively clean isn't necessary.

If He's the Problem

If your significant other is the one who's causing some tension in the living situation, try to approach the issue with the calm and respect you would hope he approaches you with. Everyone has their own way of doing things, so when you start living with someone new, you have to adapt, whether you like it or not.

"Compromise" is a word all my friends currently living with a significant other use. I mean, we have to compromise when living with a roommate, so living with your boyfriend is no different. The only thing here is that you're sharing everything with this roommate—the bed, the closet, literally anything and everything becomes available to the other person.

If there is something that he's doing that you don't like, you need to bring it up so it doesn't become a point of contention. Remember when Harry moved in with Charlotte in *Sex and the City*, and he liked to sit around, naked, on all her white furniture? Yeah.

I'll allow it.

Moving in with someone you really, really enjoy spending time with is generally thought of as being exciting. And it is! It's a good thing! (Did you read that in Ross's voice when he kept saying, "I'm fine!" because that's definitely how I said it.) Letting small things like space, or controlling the remote, or anything else miniscule and unimportant in the grand scheme of things get to you is ridiculous when you think of what you're getting in return. (A roommate, taking up your space, but we won't acknowledge that.)

You get to have the company of someone you love, and someone who loves you, and you get to have that support day and night. So, remember that when you're nitpicking everything he does that gnaws at your subconscious. Is his loud breathing reminiscent of one Darth Vader? Sure. Does he stomp around like he's got tree trunks for legs? Oh, only always. But you love it!! The importance lies with the person, not the environment.

 My Therapist Says that she agrees with me and that a step like moving in with somebody really is something to be celebrated, and focusing on things that are irrelevant will take away from that joy, so don't do it. This is a person you've come to know and love—love enough to want to fall asleep next to them and see them first thing in the morning. That's something people wish for: trying to find their own special someone. Always keep that in mind when the small things get in the way.

Because like a cellmate in prison, nothing says love like a constant companion.

Over It, TBH

In a cruel twist of injustice, you were broken up with before you could even send that pity "I'm sorry, it's not me, it's you" text. Smile, because you've just been unburdened of this gargoyle who was anchoring you to the pits of insignificance, where he roamed, undisturbed. You're free to go and conquer new heights—and Meghan Markle your way into a royal family.

Okay, so it's not that easy, but it should be. You get a three-day-mourning period, and then you are DONE. Do not, under any circumstances, and no matter how genetically cursed you are, devote any more time to this loser. He will feel it, and know that he's the one winning, and you're the one listening to Adele (Taylor Swift, John Legend, *Titanic* soundtrack, whatever) on repeat. It's been scientifically proven by the scientists here at My Therapist Says (who have no formal education, but plenty of real-life case studies) that it takes a guy about two to four weeks after a breakup to really start feeling the effects of it, whereas women suffer instantaneously, and are the first to get the fuck over it.

So, know that, right now, yes, it seems like it can't be worse and life sucks, but he will come crawling back, and it'll be up to you to decide which of the fifteen inhumane ways you'll choose to tell him to go fuck himself. This isn't bitterness, fyi; it's just science.

TAKING THE HIGH ROAD? NEVER HEARD OF IT.

If You Run into Him

If, accidentally on purpose, you happen to see him out and feel like bawling your eyes out, act so happy and #OverIt that he will start to question whether you two even dated in the first place. Relationship amnesia is the best way to remind him of his place in the hierarchy of your life. And why he broke up with you. If you're doing *this* much better without him, maybe *he* was the problem? It's all about appearances. Appear like you're not letting anything get to you, and you're so much fun, and, omg, everyone loves you! Faking it is the halfway point to actually being over it.

But if there is absolutely nothing to resuscitate you from this agonizing moment, because you're reminded of all the plans that didn't pan out, and you're questioning everything, I defer to The 3 Stages of a Breakup on the next page. My personal stages are Rage, Revenge, and Retribution. The last two may sound similar, but to me, there's a world of difference, and all the intricacies involved definitely differentiate them. But those aren't applicable for people who don't suffer from rage blackouts, so let's cover the ones that can apply to everyone.

Tip: Try to avoid drinking in this situation because you will either cry, embarrass yourself, or make him question why he dated you in the first place. Channel Elle Woods post–law degree, not Elle Woods post-salad.

The 3 Stages of a Breakup

Stage 1: Hypothetical Vengeance

- Cry/be sad/do what you need to do for three days.

- Compartmentalize your pain in a corner of your brain where you will come back to it in due time, and then start plotting a detailed plan of how to execute revenge. Be as graphic/colorful as you please!

- Write down all of his flaws to reread when second-guessing yourself and the decision.

- Write down all of your attributes to remind yourself what a catch you are and how hard it will be for him to move on. Send him love and pity vibes.

- Create a fun playlist.

- Pretend nothing happened.

I'M SORRY
I CAN'T,
I HATE YOU —

Stage 2: Do You

- Okay, so you can't forget, but you need to start going out with other people; meeting new guys, and distracting yourself, to the best of your ability.

- Every time you think of him, immediately distract yourself. Get into the habit of not thinking about him.

- Don't listen to sad music—no one likes a Debbie Downer. So, blast your Hype Playlist from Stage 1.

- Start taking super-hot pics and make your Instagram a virtual *Vogue*.

- Start doing something good for yourself, like exercise or a change of diet—anything that makes you feel better.

- Find out who your ex's enemy is. Date him. Bonus tip: Get engaged to him.

- Run into somebody who knows him (but do NOT run into him), and look really good, so it gets back to your ex how great you're doing.

- Accomplish something in your professional life so he sees how you're not only attractive but also intelligent and successful.

Stage 3: A Phoenix Rising from the Ashes (Shout-Out to Ben Affleck)

- You're wiser, worldlier, and healthier now; you barely have any anger left within you.

- Run into him after coordinating it that way, and literally take his breath away with how amazing you look. Act so above it and nice that you don't even remember any malice in the first place.

- Once he, inevitably, wants you back, get ready to execute the plan of revenge you plotted in Stage 1.

- Or just laugh in his face, as you walk away with a cooler/better/smarter/funnier guy.

EXAMPLE: Carrie running into Big while on a date with a famous New York Yankee in *Sex and the City*.

Once you've gone through all three stages, the world is your oyster. You may now proceed with the plan of vengeance that you took arduous hours creating with Napoleonic attention to detail. You might even, at this point, be so above it all, that you'll let this one slide and move on, because you have better things to do and you're mature. If you're at all like me, this will not be the case. You will ride that train straight into his demise.

Remember: #AlwaysMakeThemRegret!

My therapist is furiously shaking her head and pleading with me to remove this, but I stand by my healing process. She insists that a healing process this is not, but something more fitting to lunacy.

Is your therapist allowed to insult you? Asking for a friend.

The Win-stinct
(or Women's Intuition)

The Win-stinct is that sense of impending doom that a breakup is near and imminent, and to continue being the Taylor Vaughan of your own life, you must do it first, and swiftly. The key here is to always win; therefore . . . don't tiptoe around this like a coward. Use that #blessed intuition Mother Nature gifted you and dump his ass. My favorite way to end things? A text message: it's personal and you don't have to see them cry!

 My Therapist Says absolutely not.

Some people are born with the Win-stinct, others hone it through the changing tides of life, and some will forever roam this Earth praying for intuitive abundance to come their way. Call it women's intuition, or whatever you want, but as I stated earlier, if a girl is sensing something is off, she's usually right. I can't explain it, but somehow, women just know— like our mothers and how they're always annoyingly right, even when we don't want to admit it. If you have even the slightest inclination that it's going south, break it off first. It can only go a few ways:

    a. It opens up the conversation that something is amiss, which, I guess, is key to a healthy-ish relaysh?

    b. You were right, and he was planning on booting you like a bad first impression on *The Bachelor*.

c. You're completely wrong, and he's now confused and will doubt you for, well, ever. You can try getting out of this one by saying you heard he was going to do it first, and then lie your way through the whole thing.

Either way, trust your instincts. Take control of your destiny. Work on that Spidey sense and you will always know what's up. I am an absolute zero where Win-stinct is concerned, and I am DROWNING (metaphorically). As a hopeless case, I salute you in your quest of inner exploration.

 My Therapist Says breakups are never easy, and never truly one-sided. You may have given your all and truly believed the relationship was solid, but somehow, somewhere, your paths went separate ways. There's no one way to heal and process anguish; you just have to go with it at your own pace and remain hopeful— hopeful that, with time, this will have been a lesson, and maybe along the way, you will see why. Don't harbor anger, because it will only harm you. Doing anything from a place of anger is ill-advised. Use it as motivation, but don't use it to hinder yourself.

Ummmm, like I said, *retribution.*

When You Wish You Were Single

There are times when you'll want to break up with someone first, and you won't know how, because that person keeps threatening various things if you decide to end the relationship. This requires effort and patience on your part, because nobody wants to be stuck in a car with a crybaby who can't move on. Ugh. I know that in the previous section I said you need to grab destiny by the balls and be the initiator at your first possible convenience, but there are cases where even I'd be like, um, okay, he needs therapy. Or Jesus.

These people make it impossible to break up with them, and you feel inclined to give it some thought. Some people just have a hard time letting go, even though you've mentally and physically moved on—months ago. They can't imagine life without you (obvs) and will do anything to keep you, which, drumroll, *puh-lease* . . . begins the CYCLE.

IT'S NOT YOU, IT'S ME. I'M JUST A COACH WITH A ROSTER.

The Cycle

Nothing is worse than being in a relationship cycle of breaking up and making up. Like, get a clue: if you wanted to break up in the first place, clearly things were amiss. Popularizing the belief that it is through challenges and adversity that true love prospers is unhealthy, and quite frankly, frightening. That's kind of how abusive relationships happen, people!

Things change, circumstances change, and even people sometimes reevaluate themselves, but changing a person takes time. And energy. And patience. And whyyy should you have to put yourself through the torment and humiliation of sticking around for something that is clearly dragging you down? Not to be bummer, but *that's* a bummer. Let "Toxic" be a song by Britney, not your life motto.

I'm all about advocating for love and all its intricacies, as long as it's worth it. Most of the time, the things people stay around for are not only visibly *not* worth it, they're all around *not* worth it. Do you really want to be exchanged for a hotel? (Looking at you, Chuck Bass.) This sounds selfish, but how many friends do you wish you could knock some sense into who are staying in relationships for all the wrong reasons? Over time, that kind of behavior takes a toll on you, so you have to ask yourself, "Is it worth it?" Like a Band-Aid, pull this shit off deftly and skillfully, bearing in mind your significant other's mental state and well-being. If he's a complete clinger, bring in reinforcements.

My Therapist Says you need to tread carefully with people who seem to be having a harder time getting it and moving on, so just be patient. It's not always malicious; however, if you're noticing that it is coming from a manipulative place, or feels dangerous, extricate yourself from the situation, because prolonging the cycle can do more harm than good.

As usual, my therapist is repeating my wisdom and passing it off as her own. Just kidding. She will probably stop picking up my phone calls after she reads this.

Am I a CEO Yet?

(The Annoyances and The Obstacles)

THE CEO OF BEING THE CEO.

You say "lazy piece of shit."

I say "productively procrastinating."

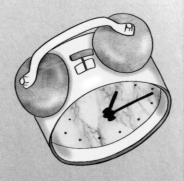

The Unbearable Boss

You're at your desk, clicking away, making it sound as though what you're doing is of great importance and actually productive, all while keeping one hand below, clutching your phone as you're scrolling through Instagram in the monotonous fashion of looking at everything with minimal attention. Visibly, you're the personification of hard work and dedication, but mentally? You're wondering when it's an acceptable time to pour a glass (bottle) of rosé. . . . Is 2 p.m. a faux pas?

We've all, at some point, been asked to do something we didn't want to do, either because it was expected of us, we had no other choice, or we somehow got stuck doing it. Whether you were being paid for it or not, you understand the strife of being so over it without having the luxury of physically being allowed to be over it.

For a lot of people, their livelihoods depend on their ability to be able to flourish in this environment, however unwilling they are. So, how do you embody the ideal worker with minimum effort, all while receiving maximum praise?

The Bare Minimum Checklist

☐ Adopt a stern or concerned facial expression that tells people you're so serious, or deep in thought; therefore, you must be figuring out an incredibly important work crisis. (Meanwhile, you're trying to figure out which type of potato you are on BuzzFeed.)

☐ Nod with said concerned/stern facial expression, while feigning impatience, as if you always have a phone call to tend to or paperwork that needs your immediate attention. This will then allow you to retreat to the security of your desk as often as possible (into the solace of *Vogue* magazine).

☐ Affect an interest in the workplace, the people, the problems; meanwhile, actually focus on your personal life.

☐ Try to avoid being seen doing anything frivolous so your austere reputation remains untarnished and the respect for you grows.

☐ Befriend the office keener (a Carol) and split your workload with your new office bestie!

☐ Take a really long time to finish each assignment, pretending you're transforming it from a normal assignment to something extraordinary. You don't actually have to make it great, but make them believe that you do everything above and beyond. With your affected confidence and stern command of the room, they'll react appropriately.

❑ Pretend to be sick every now and then while still coming into the office, showing you're a devoted worker and nothing will stop you from getting the job done.

❑ Focus on a cute guy in the office, devote your time to slowly getting to know him, and *voilà*: you've found something interesting to do, making the days go by faster (if no cuties, focus on building your life beyond the workplace).

❑ Always maintain an air of mystique.

❑ When video conferencing from home, mute yourself as you freeze your screen on a photo of you looking ENRAPTURED by what's being said. (Feel free to get creative with your Zoom background. A library, you say? From the comfort of your fortress of pillows?)

❑ If your boss is judging your performance based on your participation in a meeting, ask many time-consuming questions and repeat every smart thing someone else says, in a convoluted way.

❑ Sprinkle in these words in meetings for decorative purposes: thus, therefore, nonetheless, let's circle back, indubitably, let's digest this, don't boil the ocean, per my last email.

I guess ignore this illuminating list if you're one of those people who loves your job and finds the tasks and challenges of a new day thrilling. You do you, Carol.

When Your Boss Hates You

Dear MTS,

My boss hates me. Every morning, we have these fun, open, and relaxed meetings, where everyone blurts out ideas as they come into their heads, passing them from person to person and adding to them. Whenever I speak or contribute, my boss rolls her eyes or dismisses my idea. I don't know what to do. I've tried kissing up to her. I've tried to be confident. I don't really know what else to do. Any advice?

—Bailey

I can so relate to this. While it can seem like almost everyone slightly despises me, no one hates me more than my bosses, past and present. *It's a vibe.* I like to believe it just means that you've got something unique about you and the haters can't handle it, and are therefore incredibly jealous of you. Look, Bailey, you need to figure out, whether through the grapevine, by sleuthing, or some other more creative method, why she hates you:

- ❑ Did you date her ex?

- ❑ Do you remind her of a traumatic childhood friend/experience?

- ❑ Or are you just annoying?

You've got to ask yourself the honest and hard questions, leaving no stone unturned. Basically, you need to become a Carol. It's very hard to constantly demean a Carol because she's already so annoying and keen that she doesn't react to it, so it takes the fun out of it. She just takes it all with a smile and the upbeat attitude for which she is known, and moves on with her delusional self. By playing up your inner Carol, you're covering all your bases: you're hardworking, you're eager, you're dedicated. Once you've convinced people of your full-blown Carol status, they'll probably just try to avoid you and approach you only when they need something.

This is a good thing because, for the most part, you'll be left alone and nobody will care enough to be mean to you. No Carol has ever been threatening or posed a concern for anyone, so adopting Carol-like qualities is like wearing a lifejacket in a pool; you're just being safe. At peak Carol-status, life might seem too good to be true. Your workload will be lighter, or it will just feel that way, because the pressure is off as nobody wants to talk to you too often, so they sort of let you run off to do whatever you want. Considering how much of a loser they think you are, they trust that you won't do anything too reckless.

It is both a blessing and a curse, the power that comes with being a Carol.

If the annoyingly zealous enthusiasm isn't your thing, you can try to be aloof and unattainable (see The Bare Minimum Checklist on page 84). Just avoid getting too close to people, lest they figure out that this was all a ploy to avoid any real pressure at work. If even *that* doesn't work, consider a new career path because you have on your hands a Susan . . .

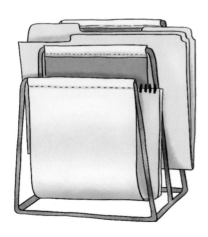

The Susan
(or What Nightmares Are Made Of)

Now, to truly understand the dynamics of the workplace, we must focus all our attention and annoyance on the antagonist of every tale: The Susan.

I briefly touched upon the infamous Susan earlier, giving you only a glimpse into the workings of the psychopathic and demonic mind of a Susan. Her blatant disregard for everyone and everything makes her as hated as she is feared. Often, she only has friends out of necessity, because this type of person doesn't require friendships to survive. And people only go along with it to placate the real-world equivalent of Voldemort that is Susan.

It (Susan) feasts on fear and insecurity, and its intuition is deceptively well honed for someone as out of touch as it is. Reading these sentences, a face(s) flashes into your mind, as we've all got a Suse to deal with (unless you are the Susan in the scenario *shudder*) and you're reminded of just how much you can't stand this person. To some, the Susan in their life is their lecherous boss, who just doesn't know when to quit, even though you've given every literal verbal cue that you are not down. To others, it's the raging CEO who knows nobody will ever be able to stand up to them, so they thrive on creating a hostile environment to test the limits of their underlings. You get the point.

Anyone can certainly pose as the Susan in your life, but for the most part, and the one I'm referring to here, is the workplace Suse. This person can be male or female, they can be old or young, they can have a bevy of traits not mentioned here, but what they all have in common is that they are not liked and incapable of READING THE ROOM. Or, you know, maybe they are and they just don't care, which is admirable, if you think about it. But their personality makes even that one attribute seem like a flaw. To truly analyze the severity of your Susan, you must first identify what type of Susan you are dealing with.

The 4 Types of Susan

SINGLE SUSAN: This type of Susan is perpetually single, so they make sure everyone gets on their level. They make you stay late, assign work on weekends/holidays, and the only time you see actual emotion from them is when it relates to their cat(s) and/or dog(s). Try having a social life on their watch! I think not. Think: Margaret Tate in *The Proposal*

ANGRY SUSAN: This type of Susan is basically a rage-oholic and has the temper of Alec Baldwin when leaving voicemails for his daughter. Do anything even marginally wrong and ready yourself for the colorful insults about to be hurled at you. Think: Ari Gold in *Entourage*

SAD SUSAN: This type of Susan is going through something. ALWAYS. So, they're perpetually feeling "some type of way," which they feel gives them the right to treat you like you are beneath them. Whether this trauma is pressing or not, they will be able to guilt you into not hating them quite as much as you should because they have been "dealing with some issues" . . . for, like, ten years now. Think: Heath in *White Chicks*

BITCHY SUSAN: This type of Susan is on a power trip and has absolutely no visible reason to be such a bitch. They are successful, have a healthy social life, and seem to have it together, but overall, they're just incredibly cruel for sport. Different from Single Susan, this type of Susan can be in a relationship. Think: Miranda Priestly in *The Devil Wears Prada*

After having identified what type of evil it is that you're dealing with, you can then spearhead the cause of getting said Susan to like you. The Susan is a delicate creature that should be approached with caution and handled with care. Every boss is different and has their own singular set of quirks. Once you've figured out how to manage your personal karmic retribution for God knows what, you can then begin mitigating the office politics with finesse and ease.

My Therapist Says she is against the term "Susan" and its negative connotations. As a therapist should be, I guess? She thinks approaching your work seriously and responsibly is what is expected of an adult, and that work ethic will reap its own reward. She also thinks identifying and focusing on your boss's negative qualities will only emphasize them and attract more with that mindset. Being positive, professional, and productive at work will lead to more opportunities, so she thinks focusing on how to deal with your "Susan" will only hinder you.

I mean, maybe, but what does she know?

Un-Employ Me
(or To Quit or Not to Quit?)

There was a study done a while back on what people who were on their deathbeds most regretted about their lives, and it was almost always a unanimous answer of "time." Wasted time, unfulfilled time, time that you're never getting back doing something you don't love. Being a product of the millennial generation, my constant advice to anyone unhappy or confused is to follow your dreams and accomplish your goals, however unrealistic they may seem. You don't want to wake up one day, thirty years from now, having dedicated so much time and energy to something you don't love, only to realize you've hardly done anything at all because you've

always put it off—for another time. You need to live a life that's entirely your own, and make mistakes, and decisions, that will make you the person you will become. Sometimes, the conventional route is the one to be avoided. If we look at history, most of the great inventions or moments have happened because somebody decided they were going to forgo convention and do it their own way.

So, if you feel like you're seemingly stuck and unable to leave a job due to the fear of financial instability, then make a game plan, with dates, time lines, budgets, and whatever else you need to execute it. Don't wait until it's too late to realize your potential. Pursue your goals by first identifying what they are, and then try to come up with a realistic way to realize them. After that, begin your path to success.

Remember: Don't be fearful and believe in yourself. Even if no one else does. Unless you're, like, auditioning for *American Idol* and literally every person you've sung to has said you should absolutely avoid that career path, probably listen to them?

 My Therapist Says my advice is pretty spot-on, until the *American Idol* thing, so I guess I can't be perfect all the time.

HATERS? OH, YOU MEAN DELUSIONAL FANS?

The Haters
(or Can You Not?)

If you're mildly attractive, with a modicum of intelligence and success, there will be people envious of you. It's just, like, the facts of life. Call them losers, delusional, rude, mean, literally anything you want, but in a word, they are HATERS.

We all have them, whether it's a teacher who predicted you would drop out of high school and not amount to much, or an ex-boyfriend who was convinced you were using your looks to get ahead (even though most people who know me would kindly say that I was an "interesting-looking" child, so looks I do not depend on). Basically, if you don't have haters, you need to step up your game. The problem isn't really why you have haters, because haters don't really need a reason. It's just how good your diplomacy is in dealing with them.

Dear MTS,

My friend was recently fired from her job and is spending all her free time complaining. She keeps trying to encourage me to be angrier, in general, at everything. I'm trying to help her get back on her feet, but it seems all she wants to do is complain. Sometimes, she'll say rude things about my job to our other friends to make a point of how I'm "putting up with it."

What can I do to help, and to get her to stop?

—Sveta

Um, let her wallow? Lol, just kidding.

Good on you, Svets, for looking out for your girl. This is a hard time for her, and she probably needs, like, a grace period of three days (yes, always only three) to get it out of her system and hate the world for its injustices. Then, she needs to pull it together and go out there to secure an even better job.

You could try giving her pep talks to rally her spirit to conquer the big, bad world. Always let her know that you're there for her, in any capacity you can be! If that doesn't work, tell her that you don't want to be around that kind of negativity. It may sound harsh, just extricating yourself from somebody's life when the going gets tough, but if they're intent on bringing you down with them, they will try to do that at all costs, no matter the situation. So, what you're really doing is self-preservation.

How to Coexist with Haters

Dear MTS,

My best friend and I have started hanging out more with our coworkers, who are rough around the edges. They'll say things that are questionable at best, like how all feminists are crazy women with hidden agendas, but they'll say it in such a way that if you don't laugh at the joke, you take yourself too seriously. Most of the time, they're nice, but comments like that will come out and cover everything from politics to relationships, and I always want to tell them to fuck off. My bestie, however, laughs along and even plays into it. I know she's not like that, and I keep telling her to stop, but she says they're just joking and that I should lighten up.

—Morgan

Ever have a knee-jerk reaction when someone opens their mouth, because you just know whatever comes out next is going to make you both metaphorically and physically violent? This is that. The people you're hanging out with sound like awful people, or like most people I've encountered, ever, so I can't judge. What I can say is that your friend is a classic case of, like, every middle-school mean girl movie ever: playing along to fit in. What does it cost her to laugh a few times here and there, if it means she's popular? These are the attributes I personally encourage in myself, and my friends. Lie to fit in. Because once you fit in, you have more of a voice that's listened to.

I know what you're thinking, but read on.

I'm not saying that you have to agree or believe what you're hearing, but often, the best way to change a systemic injustice is to infiltrate the system, and do so from within. Nobody is going to care because someone they find to be inferior told them they're being mean and wrong. That's unrealistic, unfortunately. But if one of their own stands up and acknowledges something isn't right, they'll listen. And they'll start to question things, too, beginning the conversation needed for change.

Now, we're sure your friend isn't doing this to incite a revolution, but maybe if you approach her with this idea in mind, that the power is in her hands, she will begin to consider it. We are a lot quicker to listen if we are flattered simultaneously.

You can't fault your friend for wanting to fit in and be liked. We've all done things we aren't quite proud of when impressing that certain someone, ahem, like, say, starting a petition for an endangered animal only to find out that you had misspelled and mispronounced said animal that was never endangered to begin with (overpopulated, in fact) . . . The POINT is that you need to have a chat with your friend, and if you're still unhappy, extricate yourself from the situation.

My friend Ashley liked this guy so much that she pretended to be heavily religious, like his family, to gain approval and respect from him and them. And for a while, it worked! He was charmed and in love with her, finding it unbelievable that he found a beautiful girl, who was not only nice and fun, but who also shared his uncommon religious values. That is, until he saw her out, acting anything but. Safe to say, the whispers he had been hearing that told him she was lying were true and he broke up with her on the spot. The only plus side was that she could stop pretending and go back to being her hedonistic self. So, my advice on lying? As it's always been: if you're getting away with it, mazel tov!

How to Win When Dealing with Liars

> **Dear MTS,**
>
> One of my coworkers was promoted and her position became available. I told my friend, who is also my coworker, that I wanted to submit my name for the position, and was working up the courage to do so. She encouraged me, telling me that I deserve it and I should go demand it. Well, finally I did, only to find out that she had already done it behind my back and gotten the position before me, for her "ambition," as my boss put it. Do I have a right to be mad, as technically she has every right to also want the job?
>
> —Jane

Oh, Jane. Sweet, naive, almost unbelievably so, Jane. HAVE YOU LITERALLY NO COMMON SENSE? Okay, so, right off the bat, as I read the second sentence, I knew where this was headed. Literally anyone with any survival instincts whatsoever would know where this was headed. In this day and age, it's every person for themselves. It's like the entrepreneurial Hunger Games. Have you seen *The Social Network*? Loyalty and kindness are not qualities admired in a boardroom, filled with ruthless and ambitious men looking to prove why women are of such weak mettle.

Jane, you sound like a nice girl, so I will try to address this with as much empathy as I can muster from my cold and weathered heart. Technically, yes, what your coworker did wasn't wrong. It's the way she did it that you have a right to be furious about. You trusted her and confided in her—as a friend. If she was any kind of decent person, she would have told you

I don't need a backstabbing bitch in my life—I'm doing just fine ruining it on my own.

that she had been considering doing the same, and then you two would have parted as adversaries who can at least say they respected the other's integrity . . . in a dream world. In reality, you should never confide in someone who is literally in the same position as you, looking to clamber up the social ladder to get the promotion that would benefit them. This seems simple enough.

Is it fair that just because you confided in her that she shouldn't have the same chance as you? If anything, she was smart in her approach of just going for the promotion instead of discussing it. That's the kind of gall women get criticized for not having. Does that mean she wanted it more, or deserved it more? Not necessarily, but it displays, in your boss's eyes, that she has the take-charge attitude that is respected and inspires confidence. This is a gray area, though.

Her being a shitty person and doing this behind your back, on the other hand, is duplicitous, and for that, you have every right to excommunicate this Benedict Arnold.

Putting Yourself First (Again)

By my saying putting yourself first, I'm not encouraging society to be selfish and have a blatant disregard for the people around them, although I never truly discourage that. It's probably why I've been in therapy for as long as I have. It's just that, as a woman, it is hard enough to elevate your rank at work without being called a "bitch" or any other adjectives men use to describe women with any ambition resembling their male counterparts, for fear they might actually do the job better.

In these situations, when you have an actual chance to persevere, don't discuss it, mulling it over, and giving your adversaries a chance to beat you to the punch. Instead, summon all the strength you know you have within and prove to everyone exactly why you're worthy. Didn't someone say it was better to be feared than respected? Was it a dictator? I probably shouldn't quote it.

My therapist actually twitched with a bit of pride at this advice. Or she has a nervous tic from all the years spent with me. Either way, she approves.

Oh! One more thing. Start plotting revenge on this hater and dole it out ruthlessly, giving her feelings as much regard as she gave yours.

Okay, see, my therapist disapproves of that one, quite blatantly. Sigh. You can't please everyone.

That Was *Probably* Karmic Retribution?

This leads to a question I've been asked more than once: Is karma something I believe in?

Personally, I'm probably in karmic jail, for everything I've ever said about kitten heels and people who wear them. Do I believe that harming someone, intentionally, be it verbally or whatnot, has consequences beyond the ones humans dole out themselves? Indubitably. It seems, so often with the news we read or see, that bad things happen to those who deserve it the least. And those who we wish would explode in intense flames seem to be going on with life in euphoric contentment, knowing their only critic to be themselves.

I cling to the belief that just because you can't see evidence of somebody riding the karmic tide to hell does not mean it is nonexistent. Some people are just better at hiding their misfortune, if only to prove to people that they're untouchable. At least this is a theory I tell myself and hold on to, to cope with the injustices I witness time and time again. I know. I'm, like, this modern little activist, paving the way for the good folk!

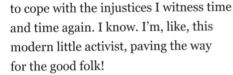

THE ONLY BIGGER BITCH THAN ME IS KARMA.

My Therapist Says you need to first observe and try to understand why somebody is doing something awful to you, before sending judgment and anger their way. It's hard to go against what you know to be right and not stand up for yourself, but the ones who are able to practice that restraint will come out on top. She believes attributing everything to karma is not the worst thing, if it makes you watch your actions and your behavior.

In my opinion, being aware of that, but still standing your ground, is the way to go. Like, I mentally don't think I'm capable of letting people get away with being haters. They need to be called out and dealt with swiftly, lest they inspire a legion of devoted followers who will, well, hate you. If history has taught us anything, it's that people seldom follow reason, but instead follow the person who sounds sure of what they're saying, and is saying it loudly, even if it's gibberish.

The Cardi B Phenomenon

For as long as I've been paying attention, I've noticed that there is a world of difference between humility and self-deprecation. Humility is often met with approving glances and a testament to your good upbringing, but self-deprecation just tends to skew insecure and kind of sad. For example, if a woman is complimented on her incredible new idea that will benefit the company she works for, she must either feign shy indifference and thank people profusely, because she is so adorable and unassuming, OR she has to sit there and list off reasons as to why she's sure it's all garbage, and how, ultimately, the idea will fail. But, it's all in good fun! Ugh. It's never just "Oh, okay, thank you!"

Why are we so unable to accept compliments without the proper amount of refusal, signifying that we are, in fact, not pieces of shit? Men seldom are guilty of this, if I am to generalize. This behavior is most often seen in women trying to come across as humble and mild mannered. And though it's appropriate in some instances, women should be able to celebrate and accept praise like their male counterparts: with confidence and agreement. Men aren't questioned when they think every mildly intelligent idea/thought that comes into their heads is brilliant or revolutionary, but women often have to justify and explain what they're doing, why they're doing it, and what the conclusion will be.

This is what we at My Therapist Says call the "Cardi B Phenomenon": when a woman has to constantly justify her place, rationalizing where she came from, why she deserves to be there, and explain it a thousand times over, only to be looked at with half the enthusiasm a man receives—like the singer Cardi B, who constantly has to acknowledge that she worked as a stripper, and is always put down because of it, with her talent and credibility questioned. Meanwhile, every male rapper with a more-than-questionable background gets to fly by for no other reason than his gender. And it is a rule that far preceded Cardi B; she's just the modern personification of it.

Often, a woman who's achieved a high level of success has to justify why she's there, time and time again, as her every decision is questioned. She will be branded emotional at any small window of weakness, because, unlike men, women make their decisions based on their emotional well-being. One misstep, and the fragile foundation on which she is standing comes crumbling down. This is true of every woman in every industry; we are always waiting for there to be failure.

We waited for Britney Spears, the perfect representation of wholesome American girl, and we did the same thing with Taylor Swift. And we will continue to wait for the rise and fall of another young newcomer, who, for a moment, makes us believe that good can prevail. Until it doesn't. We wait for every new young actress to make a misstep, just so we can nod our heads in condescension, thinking, "Told you so." We wait for the small number of women in politics to disappoint us, because ultimately, that's what we've been conditioned to expect.

That's not to take away from every hardworking man who has had his own challenges and battles to overcome, so don't vilify me just yet. (There are plenty more reasons, but this one isn't it.) There's no reason to victimize one sex in favor of the other. Unfortunately, it is a generalization that tends to be proven true, time and time again, with women playing the humility card as men play the Jordan Belfort-esque bravado, reserved for particularly revolting characters on TV.

So, to achieve Indra Nooyi–level goals, learn how to take a fucking compliment. Learn how to accept praise. Learn how to confidently pitch an idea, believing in it wholeheartedly so that it doesn't leave room for doubt. Learn the idea that belief can be the final ingredient in your recipe for success.

The Career Woman and Love

Nowadays, being a feminist can mean one of two things: Lena Dunham or everyone else. Lols, *kidding*. There are two types of feminists, though, at least in the eyes of our disapproving society. Some people's definition of a feminist is an angry woman out to get the world, breathing fire upon any man who dares glance at her a moment too long, leaving no argument unfinished, lest people start to think women the weaker sex. The other, however, is a woman who understands that feminism means not much more than equality, something that seems like it should be a basic human right—being treated equally to your male counterpart, *non*?

The first definition was, of course, created only to subdue and discourage the current waves of solidarity of womanhood from country to country, getting louder, and evidently, more frightening to men who are deeply insecure. The second is, um, like, just true. These days, if you're even remotely successful at your job, you're almost expected not to have an equally successful relationship, because God forbid you balance the two and not prioritize the man!

I've heard stories ranging from boyfriends feeling like they're not getting the amount of love and attention that they usually expect, to stories where girls are interrupted mid-meeting because Romeo decided to post up after a few missed texts.

Hint: Those texts will, without fail, come from the type of guy who will stand in line for two days to audition for *The Bachelor* if given the chance.

A RELATIONSHIP AND A CAREER? WHAT, LIKE IT'S HARD?!

So, what do you do from here? Do you sacrifice your career for a husband, a family, and all that fun? Don't start hating me now thinking I don't respect being a mother as I do a career woman, because that's not the case. If that's been a dream of yours or you really are just that maternal, that's amazing and you'll probably make an incredible CEO of a household. Also, adopt me??? But, if you did it only to fit in to the ideals placed for you by history and society, then you're doing yourself and all the women who've fought for your rights a disservice. Even though it seems hard at first, paving your own path should be respected, admired, and supported. This isn't just on the women, either, because it ultimately comes down to both sexes to further this cause.

That said, any man who can be classified as a decent human being should have no qualms with this as it doesn't directly insult or take away anything from him, but only provides the same treatment for the opposite (fairer) sex.

Regretting Your Success Because You're Single

Dear MTS,

I'm nearing the age of thirty-six, and I realized I've accomplished so much in my career that I completely disregarded my love life. It seems like it's only now dawning upon me that my best years are behind me, and I have to settle. The thought is driving me to depression, because in my career, I believe that you never settle until you get exactly what you want. And I'm wondering now whether I placed my priorities in the wrong order, because when I come home to my beautiful, big apartment, I'm coming home alone.

—Michelle

These are the kind of blanket statements that infuriate me, because who exactly decided a woman's "best years" were her twenties? Sure, they're our experimental and rebellious years by some definition, and the first foray into adulthood, but I've yet to hear from my friends in their thirties and forties that they wish they could turn back time to experience that discovery, heartbreak, and agony all over again. The example I'll keep coming back to about ageism is: JLO. NEED. I. SAY. MORE.

Michelle, you sound like somebody to be admired. Against all odds and voices that constantly tell women to pursue one path, you dominated the one less ventured. It may seem like it's too late to date voraciously and recklessly, like you're in your twenties, and experience the emotions you feel you may have missed out on due to your determination to succeed at work, but that's only by your decision. You are now stable and independent, so you can have all those experiences with the security blanket people in their twenties can only dream of.

You're now accomplished as a woman; you know your worth, you know your attributes, and you seem to certainly know your weaknesses, so not only are you at the beginning of an incredibly exciting time, but you're like too young for even season 1 of *Sex and the City* in the age department.

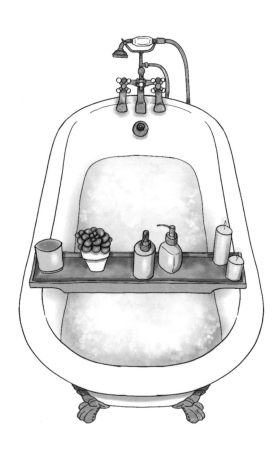

Are You a Feminist? Checklist

❑ Y ❑ N   Do you believe women should be paid equally to men, when doing the same job?

❑ Y ❑ N   Do you think women should have equal opportunities, in every field, as their male counterparts?

❑ Y ❑ N   Do you believe men should be judged as harshly as women when doing something society typically frowns upon?

❑ Y ❑ N   Should women be regarded the exact same way as men are in regard to their sex/romantic life?

❑ Y ❑ N   Should women have the option of having a choice, the way men do, in every area of their life, without being belittled or degraded for it?

❑ Y ❑ N   Do you believe in equality, always, and forever?

Literally, none of those you should've said NO to, so, guess what? You're a feminist.

Why You Are a Feminist (Including the Mallories of the World)

I think everyone can agree to the fact that any woman who, with the determination and drive typically seen in men, pursues a career successfully, is a feminist, whether she identifies with the word or not. On the other hand, my friend Mallory is convinced she's the opposite of the word "feminist" in every and any definition of the word, contributing to the regression of women in power. Those words have actually left her mouth on more than one occasion.

I know what you're thinking: at least she's incredibly self-aware. By her definition, her not having a job, goals, innate talent, or any type of prospect whatsoever, paired with her dream of being a wife/mother, is a failure to women everywhere and the embodiment of anti-feminism. But here's what I say to my Mal and the Mallories of the world: even though you may not have career aspirations, that doesn't make you anti-feminist.

Mallory is one of the first girls to come to the aid of any female being insulted or degraded in most of our conversations or public outings, and she is fiercely protective of her right to make decisions as liberally as a man when speaking of her sexual proclivities. Her lack of career, or ambition, it seems, has planted a deep-rooted seed of insecurity in her brain and she's adding to the anti-feminist narrative because she feels like she's not contributing to society in a conducive way.

But there are many ways of doing something, and if the "traditional" way isn't something that you're finding affinity in, then proceed with doing things your way. Channel your inner Erin Brockovich, and don't stop at good enough. Maybe you're doing your part at home, or within your friend group, or in your mindset; all those moments can contribute to a greater good if you believe in your abilities and yourself as a woman of worth.

Why We All Need to Be Feminists

How can women encourage and enforce the masses to denounce the misogyny and prejudices in the workplace and home front when they're incapable of implementing it among their own sex? By denouncing feminism, you're saying to all the naysayers that as a woman there is something to be said for a lack of equality in the playing field. And if that is the case, who hurt you? For real, though, you are setting us back and making yourself look completely insensitive to women and incredibly idiotic to men who applaud your ignorance. Come ON. You don't have to like us, but at least like yourself. Like yourself enough to inspire respect in a man instead of being a target.

But if you feel that you've done your research and you absolutely can't stand seeing a woman treated not even respectfully, but equally, to her male counterpart, then I suppose no more can be said. On to the women not suffering from Stockholm syndrome or any of its various contemporaries.

My Therapist Says she is actually on board with this section, being a champion of feminism and a believer that it will only lead to positive changes for women. She says that being a woman is a complicated thing, and that we must be fair to ourselves. We cannot forgo our own wishes and needs for others', as we're often told. It will lead to more havoc than good, building within us anger, resentment, and regret. And regret is the worst thing to have to carry, because you can't turn back time. So, she suggests making the most of every situation, enjoying yourself and your time, and being helpful and kind when possible. As long as you know what you need and go get it, everything else will fall into place.

If you actually read all that ↑, then bravo, 'cause I fell asleep after the second sentence. My God, the woman can go on.

Mercury's in Retrograde, I'm Texting My Ex.

(The Astrology)

On a scale of 1 to introducing your dog as a "Gemini vegetarian," how obsessed are you with astrology?

Blame It on the Stars

Since the dawn of time, people have needed to figure out why people are the way they are, and for the majority, that is, why are people so fucking annoying? Yes, there's psychology to help us out with this (and I am a shining example of the wonder of it), but more importantly, there's astrology. Seriously. It is considered an honorary social science to some. Those "some" also tell you to put a crystal on your hand to heal a broken bone, but I'll choose to look past that and be open-minded, for once.

Astrology is one of those things to which some people either attribute every factor that makes up a person or just find it to be as annoying and ridiculous as healing crystals and full-moon rituals.

Example: You like a guy, and everything seems to be going okay, but all of a sudden, he stops texting as frequently, and randomly takes a trip to Vegas. Most people would say he's a douche, but an astrology enthusiast would say he's an Aquarius. *See? Science.*

Real astrology is so much more than just what day you were born (aka your sun sign). All twelve planets and signs go into making up your personality. People say that they don't believe in astrology because those daily horoscopes from magazines/newspapers/apps don't ever match them. And that's true, as those are rarely accurate, targeting the masses and made to be as relatable as possible. The study of astrology is an ancient science, so it's hard to say whether if it's completely inaccurate, but basing all your hopes on it is also ridiculous because so many factors make up a person: nature versus nurture, their experiences, their failures, their upbringing, etc. I suggest having fun with astrology and not taking it too seriously. Investing yourself obsessively in anything is dangerous and stupid, so don't do it.

This is coming from a girl who religiously avoids anyone who happens to be a Gemini.

I'm not about to culturally appropriate and put on a Gatsby-esque gem turban, while reading out how the planets aligned on the date of your birth. I have, however, broken down the main characteristics, planets, and generalizations of each sign. *Somewhere, Neil deGrasse Tyson just felt a shiver run up his spine.* The people who know me well know there is little I love more than generalizing. Don't worry, I advised an astrologer, so my prejudices against signs who've wronged me are excluded here (for the most part).

My therapist has absolutely no comment on this chapter, lol.

The Four Elements

The elements represent the way your sign is perceived. For example, a "fire" sign is typically known to be "hotheaded," acting before thinking. While you and I may describe that as dumb and reckless, a fiery temper is typical of those whose sign falls under the fire element, exemplifying their so-called "explosive nature."

A well-balanced natal chart (aka personality) will have a healthy mix of all four elements, but that's not usually the case; often, there is a dominant element ruling a person's chart. Pay close attention, as this element is what you'll come to blame every awful choice on. I would personally say my chart is all sorts of unhealthy, with probably every fire sign and two water signs for when I start to really feel the effects of my poorly thought out actions, but I digress. These are the four element groups to which your sign belongs:

Air

SIGNS: Aquarius, Gemini, Libra

TRAITS: Detached, too cool to care, intellectual, analytical, social, confusing, prone to a white lie(s), flighty, bores easily

Earth

SIGNS: Capricorn, Taurus, Virgo

TRAITS: Loyal, hardworking, often seen as boring, materialistic, conservative, traditional, motivated, ambitious, controlling, manipulative

Fire

SIGNS: Aries, Leo, Sagittarius

TRAITS: Emotional, driven, ostentatious, natural leader, passionate, temperamental, idealistic, creative, bossy

Water

SIGNS: Pisces, Cancer, Scorpio

TRAITS: Super emotional, whiny, sensitive, moody, extremely secretive, vengeful, intuitive, caring, possessive, suspiciously private

Sun Signs
(or Your Core Values and Traits)

I am . . . so genuinely unlikable, but I won't blame that on astrology. Years of trauma and unexplored insecurity contribute to that, but my being an earth sign certainly doesn't help, you know? The overly analytical, overly critical nature of my sign piles on to my already complicated, Rubik's Cube–esque persona. If, like me, you appreciate the ability to blame almost anything, and everything, on something, or someone, astrology is your new bestie. Your sun sign, for the most part, is said to describe your internal self, traits, and values. It makes up your personality, along with your rising sign, your moon sign, and your many other alignments.

You're late to meet your friends and they start a second group chat, sans you, criticizing you for your careless, laissez-faire approach? Blame it on your "air sign." It's not your fault you were born with your head in the clouds, and their judgment is #airphobic. Now, let's find out which signs we can use as excuses. . . .

Capricorn ♑

December 22 – January 19 | Ruled by Saturn | "CEO of the Zodiac"

Women: Capricorn women are considered to be the most hardworking and ambitious in astrology. They are self-sufficient, rational, and logical. They tend to come across as classy and conservative and like the finer things in life; basically, you can always find them online shopping. For anything. Since they are ruled by Saturn (aka the wet-blanket planet that sucks the fun out of literally anything), Capricorn women can come across as extra frigid and boring/serious. As they grow older and more successful, they tend to lighten up, and, dare I say, develop a biting sense of humor?

They are usually successful at whatever career they choose. They are so ambitious and driven that relationships often come second for them. They don't feel right or ready unless they have achieved some success in their chosen field, which is a good precedent for everyone to follow. They tend to have many acquaintances but keep their circle very small, as they don't have the time or patience for silliness. They are attracted to successful, driven men. If they think their man needs them by his side to succeed, they will put their all into helping him. They are great, nurturing mothers and extremely devoted partners. They don't mind their men getting the attention, as long as their common goals are being achieved.

At their best, they are goal-oriented, traditional, loyal, and make great CEOs—they're basically like a low-key bad bitch at the core. At their worst, they can be rigid, obsessive, and calculating.

THINK: Kate Middleton, Michelle Obama, Mary Tyler Moore, Nigella Lawson, Gabby Douglas

Men: Much like their female counterparts, Capricorn men are incredibly serious and driven. In fact, they probably won't have time for you while they're pursuing their goals. They may come across as cold, boring, or unaffected, but in reality, they are usually afraid of failure and losing what they worked so hard to get. They are definitely the strong, silent, seemingly cold type, but upon devoting themselves to one woman, they become almost docile, loving, and subservient.

Capricorn men are all in their own heads, and they have a very hard time processing emotions, so they just overanalyze situations over and over, until they've exhausted themselves. They love it when women play

125

hard to get, as it excites their ambitious and driven nature. Once they fall for you, that's it; they are incredibly possessive. Often, when they finally get the girl, they are so overwhelmed with emotion, which they, obvs, can't handle, they start acting really weird and may go MIA to figure their shit out in peace.

At their best, they are the perfect example of the ideal husband who we see in movies, embodying both protective and comforting traits that women love. At their worst, they are so used to struggling and working hard that they don't know how to enjoy the fruits of their labor.

THINK: John Legend, Eddie Redmayne, Ryan Seacrest, Justin Trudeau, Elvis Presley

Aquarius ≈

January 20 – February 18 | Ruled by Uranus |
"Love me, but leave me alone."

Women: Aquarius women pride themselves on being unique and unlike anyone else. They're usually very witty and worldly, with the ability to discuss a myriad of subjects because they are fascinated by the world and people. They are known for acting too cool to care and are detached, from anything and everything. The thing is, they care *a lot*; they just aren't emotionally equipped to show people that.

They want to be free, so anyone who suffocates them with possessiveness is a deal breaker. These women rarely ever follow the crowd, preferring to do their own thing, and they don't really care who joins them. Aquarius women take their sweet time settling down. They prefer to get to know someone, seeing if that person can be trusted—they need a lover and a friend. To keep them, you'll need to possess excellent conversational skills. Nothing makes an Aquarius fall faster than long, deep talks under the moon. If you bore her, she will move on to the next one.

At their best, they are loyal, fascinating, always on the move, and respectful. At their worst, they are cold, unpredictable, selfish, and can't be bothered.

Men: Stay away! Just kidding, I guess . . . or proceed at your own discretion. Seriously, Aquarius men are hard to understand and even harder to handle, but make the greatest friends. As friends, they will always be there for you, acting as your biggest cheerleader and ardent supporter. They keep things fun and enjoy being the center of attention in their friend group.

Male Aquarians get excited at the prospect of being in a relationship, but the reality of their choice hits them fast, and they start acting out like rebellious kids. The problem is that they think they want one thing, but in reality, an entirely different thing would make them happier, but they're almost as stubborn as Tauruses, so it takes them forever to realize this (if ever). They are independent and free spirits, but they are nearly impossible to deal with if you expect any semblance of normalcy. In fact, these guys are great for long-distance relationships or open relationships, so pack yourself an Aquarius and head on over to Utah! Once things get serious, these guys can't always handle it and start to self-sabotage. You will need a lot of patience to work out whatever these guys are going through.

At their best, they are inspiring, fascinating, romantic, exciting, and imaginative. At their worst, they are selfish, childish, arrogant, and easily confused by emotions, often acting out by cheating.

TEARS STREAMING DOWN ENTIRE FACE

I'M TOTALLY FINEEEEE

Pisces

February 19 – March 20 | Ruled by Neptune | "But how does that make me feel?"

Women: Pisces women are known to be ultrasensitive, so watch what you say around them. They are extremely emotional and intuitive to other people's moods and feelings, and have a dreamlike quality that makes others around them (especially men) want to take care of them. Because they are so sensitive, they can break down easily. Not many people can handle being with someone who's always moody and needs to be constantly coddled.

Female Pisceans are very gentle and romantic, and if they care about you, they give it their all. These women are eternally faithful and devoted. Their incredible creativity, sensitivity, and ability to access their emotions make them very talented in artistic fields.

At their best, they are romantic, kind, patient, selfless and nonjudgmental, as well as incredibly spiritual and funny. At their worst, they are annoying, whiny, and unable to deal with the realities of life—a certain amount of fragility can be attractive, but this sign takes it to the next level.

THINK: Rihanna, Eva Mendes, Elizabeth Taylor, Drew Barrymore, Sharon Stone, Olivia Wilde

Men: You know those guys who think every girlfriend is the love of their life? Yeah, that would be a Pisces man. They're hypersensitive, romantic, and in love with love. They're just as emotional as Pisces women, but sometimes, honestly, even more so. It's all or nothing with them, so they can, and will, overstay their welcome in a bad relationship because there is a certain element of delusion, or "seeing the best in people."

If you're dating a Pisces guy, you need to tread very carefully. His feelings might get hurt, even if you don't mean it. You're dating a puppy, okay? If they do something wrong and their partner confronts them about it, Pisces men will immediately feel attacked and go on the offensive, since their sensitivity sees everything as a personal affront. They tend to literally never let go. If you let them, they will go back and forth with you for years, so, um, good luck.

At their best, they are sweet, romantic, loving, and affectionate, and pick up on your feelings right away. At their worst, they are overly sensitive, moody, and vengeful, and can't take any constructive criticism. Basically, the human equivalent of a Kleenex.

THINK: Justin Bieber, Steve Jobs, Stephen Curry, Johnny Cash, Kurt Cobain, Bruce Willis

Aries ♈

March 21 – April 19 | Ruled by Mars | "Winning is everything!"

Aries is the first sign of the zodiac, and rightfully so, as people born under this sign are known to be trailblazers in everything they do. They are fiery, competitive, and unrelenting. You don't want to cross them, as their anger is quick and swift, but just as quickly, they forget too.

Women: Aries women are often quite athletic thanks to all that Mars energy, so they can be good at any sport or game they try. For them, winning isn't everything—it's the only thing. They are great at technology, video games, and anything that is fun and requires some figuring out. They are straightforward and will say exactly what's on their minds, whether the other person wants to hear it or not. This might be one of the reasons why it's hard for them to keep female friendships.

They're the type who gets along better with the guys (see The Guy's BFF on page 159).

When in love, they are passionate, impulsive, and emotional. They give it their all and feel very hurt if their effort isn't reciprocated. They want a fair partnership. Actually, they quite like *everything* to be fair. They expect to have the best jobs, best relationships, and more adventures than the rest. Aries women need a partner who can keep up and not bore them or get intimidated by them.

At their best, they are exciting, loyal, goal-oriented, and successful. At their worst, they are sulky, overly competitive, blunt, and harsh.

THINK: Sarah Jessica Parker, Lady Gaga, Mariah Carey, Kate Hudson, Reese Witherspoon

Men: Aries men are a lot like Aries women: very straightforward. If they like you, you'll know. They are fun and exciting to be around because they just want to have fun and enjoy life, so they want you to be down for an adventure. They are very confident, whether that confidence is warranted or not. It's hard to withstand an Aries man's pursuit, because when they want you, they go all-out. They'll be loyal, and they will want to show you off, but you have to be super confident, confusing, and exciting to get him to this point.

Aries males can often appear selfish, as they have a bit of an "out of sight, out of mind" thing going on, but never maliciously. If you're in their physical presence, they will be all over you and treat you like a queen. But, they have lives and they're busy accomplishing things, so even if you're on their mind, they may not get around to messaging you or calling you right away. Usually, it's just a quick check-in to set the next date.

At their best, they are ambitious, strong, exciting, and always there for their loved ones. At their worst, they are selfish, callous, impulsive, and rude.

THINK: James Franco, Robert Downey Jr., Alec Baldwin, Eddie Murphy, Eric Clapton, Seth Rogen

Taurus ♉

April 20 – May 20 | Ruled by Venus | "Feed me and don't argue with me."

♀ **Women:** Taurus women are creatures of comfort, luxury, and femininity. They like to be spoiled and adored, in an old-fashioned, idealistic way, both materialistically and physically. They need their lover's undivided attention and loyalty. Amazing food, luxurious surroundings, and nice things are a necessity for them to lead a normal life. Yes, that is what they consider "normal."

Female Taureans are sensible, though, and patient, and extremely loyal to the ones they love. They can be hardworking, but only if they're motivated and are interested in whatever they're doing. They can showcase moments of intense laziness, self-indulgence, and entitlement, but usually these moments pass quickly and then they are back to being sweet and dependable. One thing they cannot deal with is change. It takes a while to anger a Taurus woman, but once you have crossed that line, she will lose it on you, and you will regret ever crossing her.

At their best, they are nurturing, creative, affectionate, and sensual. At their worst, they are lazy, selfish, and stubborn.

THINK: Audrey Hepburn, Jessica Alba, Melania Trump, Gal Gadot, Queen Elizabeth II, Gigi Hadid, Adele, Megan Fox

♂ **Men:** Taurus men are creatures of habit. They despise change of any kind, which makes them known as loyal lovers. (Good luck getting rid of a Taurus guy!) They have a reputation for being boring, but that's just them being reliable. They're the quintessential "nice guy"; you may not want to date them, but you should marry them.

They have simple needs: feed them great food, love them, and they are forever yours. (Lols, okay, so that's in its simplest form, but you get the point.)

Inherently, they are workaholics and excellent providers. They have a taste for the finer things in life, just like Taurus women, so they don't mind working extra hard to have nice things. They are stubborn and set in their ways. Once they decide they want a person, they don't give up in their pursuit.

At their best, they are charming, sweet, loyal, consistent, and generous. At their worst, they are lazy, stubborn, and spoiled.

THINK: Mark Zuckerberg, Dwayne "The Rock" Johnson, Henry Cavill, Channing Tatum, George Clooney, David Beckham, Enrique Iglesias

Gemini ♊

May 21– June 20 | Ruled by Mercury | "The Shadiest of Them All"

Women: Known to be spontaneous, flighty, and noncommittal, these women are the definition of excitement. Gemini women are quick-witted and intelligent; they can do anything they set their minds to. Their key is just not getting bored. They are curious about the world and can wear many different masks, so getting to know the real them isn't easy. In order to keep their interest, you need to always be one-upping them and staying one step ahead. That way, they are in a constant state of adventure, which is just how they like it.

Gemini women usually have a lot of friends and don't miss a party. Always on the move, these women need constant entertainment and mental stimulation. They have many personalities in one, which makes them seem untrustworthy and shady, but they revel in their own shadiness. Emotions are not their strong suit; they are the typical Manic Pixie Dream Girls.

At their best, they are seductive, exciting, witty, the life of the party, and full of energy. At their worst, they are flaky, inconsistent, anxious, and constantly confused.

Men: And the award for the wittiest assholes goes to these guys! It's hard to find a woman who has not been charmed by a Gemini guy at least once. What do I mean by that? Oh, just that when you meet a dashing, hilarious, intelligent guy who makes you feel like everything is about to change for the better . . . he is probably a Gemini. These guys are so witty, charming, and fun to talk to that you don't even realize you've already fallen for the devil. Too bad, though, because the second the pursuit is over, they tend to get bored.

Gemini men need constant mental stimulation—a really deep, intellectual conversation will be enough to catch their interest. They want the unattainable: the constant chase (see page 16). If you learn to beat them at their own game and outmaneuver them, they make great boyfriends.

At their best, they are loyal, caring, smart, and social—you want to introduce them to your friends ASAP because they can get along with anybody and make you look good. At their worst, they are inconsistent, shady, cheaters, and emotionally draining—they'll ghost you and then pop back in; it's a cycle with them that just depends on how bored they are.

OH, SO YOU'RE A GEMINI? SHOULD I RUIN MY LIFE NOW OR LET YOU DO THE HONORS?

Cancer ♋

June 21 – July 22 | Ruled by the Moon | "Fragile: Handle with Care"

Cancers have a mixed reputation. People don't tend to feel as strongly about them as they do about Scorpios or Geminis, but since Cancer is a water sign, things can get murky. Cancer women are considered to be the "Mothers of the Zodiac." It's the only sign ruled by the moon, and the moon is responsible for our emotions. So, right off the bat, you can tell that they are of the emotional variety. Free therapy!

Women: Cancer women tend to feel things first and then logically think about them later. They are known as being one of the most loyal signs. They truly are great nurturers, and mothering comes naturally for them. You typically won't find them being selfish. They are patient and loving, if you can deal with the mood swings. They literally change their moods with the phases of the moon. It seems exhausting to be them, what with all the upswings and downswings.

The good outweighs the bad in many cases, though. As far as water signs go, I'd rank them above Pisces but below Scorpio.

At their best, they are alluring, nurturing, sensitive, and very loyal. At their worst, they can be jealous, manipulative, moody, depressive, and destructive.

THINK: Meryl Streep, Selena Gomez, Margot Robbie, Ariana Grande, Lindsay Lohan, Mindy Kaling, Pamela Anderson

Men: Cancer men are full of hidden emotions and cryptic meanings. They are cool and fun as friends, but the second they fall in love, they turn into someone else. Their deep insecurities come out, and they become obsessive, suspicious, and manipulative.

Male Cancers are very compassionate and giving, so they need a partner who's sensitive to their insecurities and won't push them over the edge. These are not the guys you should ever try to make jealous or feel threatened because they physically will not be able to handle that. If you treat them with love and respect (basically have a mature relationship/do everything I've advised you not to do), they will be the best boyfriends and/or husbands.

At their best, they are generous, affectionate, sensitive to your needs, protective, and passionate. At their worst, they are miserable to be around, distrusting of everyone around them, and moody af.

THINK: Tom Cruise, Elon Musk, Tom Hanks, Harrison Ford, Benedict Cumberbatch, 50 Cent

Leo

July 23 – August 22 | Ruled by the Sun | "I will die if I'm not the center of attention."

Women: Leo women are known to be attention whores. That's why so many of them are in the entertainment industry. They are socialites, and love being in the know and known. They laugh the loudest, dress in the most attention-grabbing way (*see also:* J.Lo in the Versace dress), and seem almost uncomfortably comfortable with attention. These women need to be adored, worshipped, and showered with praise, gifts, and flattery. It's not necessarily a negative trait, since Leos are just as generous in return.

A Leo woman will do anything for love; they were born to love and be loved. They're those annoying girls who can't stay single for longer than a month and every guy they date is "THE ONE." It's fun to have a Leo woman

I'M SORRY THAT PEOPLE ARE JEALOUS OF ME, BUT I CAN'T HELP IT THAT I'M A LEO.

on your team because you'll always know where the coolest parties are, and she will let you borrow her cute clothes . . . if you can deal with the constant narcissism.

At their best, they are gregarious, full of love and life, have large groups of friends, and are generally very loyal to those they love. At their worst, they can be very jealous and live to steal attention from everyone around them, even if it's not on purpose.

THINK: Jennifer Lawrence, Madonna, Meghan Markle, Demi Lovato, Jennifer Lopez, Mila Kunis, Kylie Jenner, Coco Chanel, Martha Stewart

Men: I read somewhere that you don't know what being loved is like unless you've been loved by a Leo man. From personal experience, I definitely agree with that statement. Leo men are the most ardent lovers in the way they know how to make a girl feel special—basically a perfect boyfriend, if you're into that smothering type of love. Once these guys commit, they are loyal to a fault. They shower their friends and girlfriends with presents and their presence. These guys are outgoing, confident, and ambitious. They really feel like there's nothing they can't achieve.

Leo is a fixed sign (just like Taurus, Scorpio, and Aquarius), which means that once a Leo man chooses a mate, that's it: he thinks you belong to him even after a breakup. They can get clingy and annoying, though, so good luck if you like your space. They want to show off whoever they're dating, so be prepared to be his arm candy. Leos are quite popular, so there's always an event or a wedding to go to as his date.

At their best, they are generous with everything, including their feelings, friends, finances, and anything else that is important to them. At their worst, they are overly idealistic, don't know how to handle failure, can seem arrogant, and often tend to overstay in bad situations.

THINK: Tom Brady, Roger Federer, Chris Hemsworth, Daniel Radcliffe, Barack Obama, Ben Affleck, James Corden, Steve Carell

Virgo ♍

August 23 – September 22 | Ruled by Mercury | "I can fix that."

Women: You will never meet someone who loves making lists as much as a Virgo woman. These women have an obsessive need to be organized, which is entertaining, unless you live with one. They also love to know everything, about everything. Their diligence and studiousness in life will take their research to new levels of obsessive when they decide to take up a new subject. They're even obsessive about being obsessive. Virgos clean for fun and as a form of relaxation. Everything must be their way, or they will nitpick you to death. They are never truly satisfied with anything because of their intense need for perfection; therefore, nothing is good enough . . . including you. Everything is a project to them.

Female Virgos don't like surprises or changes, unless they're the ones who meticulously planned each detail of said surprise or change. Maybe these qualities are the reason behind their professional success; they simply get shit done and are highly intelligent and good at business. They need to constantly be in motion, doing something, being useful. Idleness irritates them. Dating a Virgo woman is awesome if you like being criticized constantly and feeling inadequate from the harshness of her words. This isn't done out of maliciousness, though, they just want everything to be perfect. Tough love is a type of love, I guess. Though they may not outwardly show it, they are incredibly competitive.

At their best, they are loyal, quick, helpful, warm, funny, intelligent, hardworking, and decisive. At their worst, they are overbearing, shy, cruel, overly critical of themselves and everyone else, bitchy, and bossy.

THINK: Beyoncé, Blake Lively, Mother Theresa, Cameron Diaz, Salma Hayek, Jada Pinkett Smith, Alexis Bledel, Taraji P. Henson

He gave me annotated thoughts about our first date and tips to improve my résumé. I really need to stop dating Virgos.

Men: Virgo men are just as critical and analytical as Virgo women, but they usually have a gentler approach. They question and overanalyze everything in their lives. They always think that things are too good to be true. Though deeply insecure, they hide it well. Virgo men are traditionalists; they take pride in taking care of the ones they love. It takes forever to earn their trust, but once you have it, there's nothing they won't do to make sure you're happy. Just don't expect a lot of excitement.

Male Virgos are just as ambitious as Capricorn men, but they tend to need more encouragement and support. They second-guess themselves a lot, so they need a lot of reassurance, even if they don't show it. They are prone to changing their minds if they are not reassured all the time.

At their best, they are highly intelligent, successful, faithful, and thoughtful. At their worst, they will drive you insane with their criticism, inability to just enjoy life, and overanalyzing of every little mundane detail.

THINK: Prince Harry, Michael Jackson, Idris Elba, Warren Buffett, Hugh Grant, Adam Sandler, Chris Pine

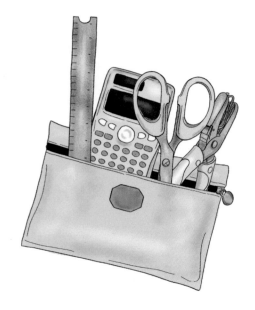

Libra

September 23 – October 22 | Ruled by Venus | "I'm not that shallow."

Women: Libra women are the tastemakers of the zodiac. If you want a good makeup or hair artist, make sure it's a Libra. Libras are ruled by Venus, the planet of all things beautiful. Kim Kardashian, the patron saint of all glam squads, is a Libra, so that should tell you everything. Their love of all things beautiful and luxurious makes them seem quite shallow, even compared to fellow Venus-ruled Taurus.

Because they're an air sign, Libras are naturally social and curious. They usually have a lot of friends who are quick to help them if and when times get tough. These women pride themselves on being fair and diplomatic, trying to avoid confrontation at all costs, so it's really no surprise that they are rather popular. They try to keep everyone on their good side, because you never know when someone can turn out to be useful to this master social climber. Libra women can be indecisive, so they prefer a strong, successful man to protect them from having to make the difficult decisions in life. In return, they will create a haven at home for their loved ones.

At their best, they are loving, fun to be around, fair, bewitching to look at, and popular. At their worst, they are scheming social climbers, backstabbing to get where they need to be.

THINK: Gwyneth Paltrow, Gwen Stefani, Serena Williams, Kate Winslet, Hilary Duff, Naomi Watts, Cardi B, Kim Kardashian

Men: Libra men are quite different from Libra women. Yes, they also enjoy beautiful things and people, but they are more verbal. They love and need to communicate. A lot. They love to talk about their feelings, and are surprisingly quick to make a move. Out of all the men of the zodiac, Libra men are probably the quickest to decide to marry someone. I know it sounds odd, seeing how indecisive they are in every other aspect of their lives, but that's probably why they usually want to marry a strong-willed woman who will help them make decisions.

They hide their sensitivity behind a wall of humor, but trust me, everything you say will be noted and remembered. Once a Libra man has zeroed in on you as his chosen partner, whether you want it or not, he will not relent. Even when rejected by their chosen object, they will stick around as friends and try to win over the object of their desire by being useful and loyal. When they like you, they will value your opinion, and you will know this because they will be sure to call you all the time to discuss anything and everything. They really do make great partners if you keep them on their toes.

At their best, they are generous, witty, loyal, and communicative, and have excellent taste. At their worst, they can be fickle and indecisive, and they love to talk about themselves and hold grudges.

THINK: Eminem, Zac Efron, Will Smith, Ryan Reynolds, John Krasinski, Lil Wayne, John Mayer, Simon Cowell

Scorpio ♏

October 23 – November 21 | Rules by Mars/Pluto | "I'm really not that crazy!"

Women: Scorpio women are usually known as being promiscuous. Even if they aren't, they appear that way because they are constantly surrounded by men. They innately know how to seduce. They are mysterious and magnetic, but be careful not to cross them. There is nothing like a Scorpio woman scorned. They will stop at nothing to get revenge if they feel betrayed or wronged. These women know what they want and how to get it. They are known to be loyal to those they love. If they love you, whether as a friend or more, they will think they own you. If their trust and their hearts are on the line, they will suspiciously watch you (emphasis on

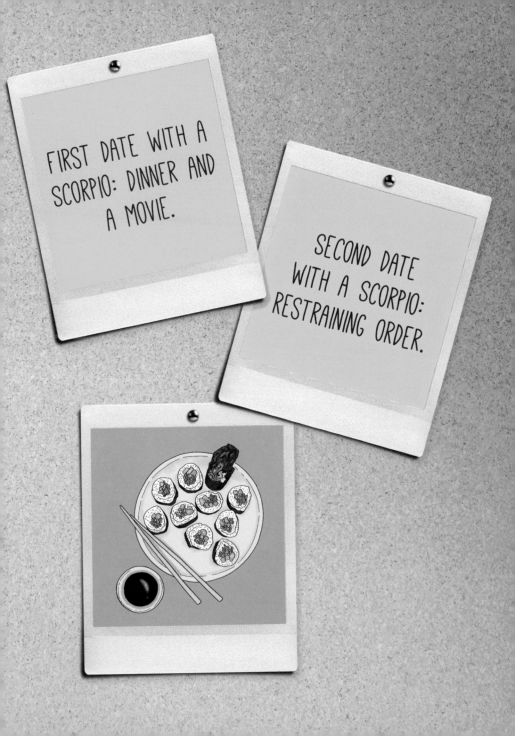

the word "suspiciously") and wait for you to fuck up. Their jealousy is the stuff of legends.

They can't process hurt without self-destructing or scorching everything around them (they aren't above setting your car on fire if you cheat on them), so they try to avoid it as much as possible by not letting many people in. Scorpio women develop an impenetrable shell after getting hurt. Once they have had enough of your nonsense, they're gone. It takes a lot to get them to this breaking point, however, because they are loyal and fixed by nature. Scorpio women need a strong man who can tame them.

At their best, they are warm, smart, and ambitious, and always get what they want. At their worst, they can be jealous of not only lovers, but also friends, and are prone to brooding and dark moods.

THINK: Julia Roberts, Emma Stone, Scarlett Johansson, Winona Ryder, Katy Perry, Rachel McAdams, Demi Moore, Ciara

Men: I don't think there is a sign as polarizing as the Scorpio male: people either love them or hate them. Depending on his maturity level, a Scorpio man can either uplift you or destroy you. He does not know the meaning of the word "chill." Scorpio is the most intense of all water signs, and Scorpio men are capable of having really deep feelings, intense passion, and unconditional love. But the only condition is, don't break their trust.

If you thought Scorpio women were known to be crazy jealous, male Scorpios are not far behind. They really can't handle betrayal of any kind. Because it takes them so long to let you in, they will be shattered if you use that trust against them. They really do love to be the brooding, silent type, and will expect you to know why they're brooding. They're complex in the way that they have a lot of double standards. They are ambitious and will stop at nothing to achieve the success they think they deserve. They are all-or-nothing. Love or hate. Nothing in between. That kind of passion can be attractive, depending on your personality.

At their best, they are intense, passionate, loyal, deep, intuitive, and amazing. At their worst, they are suspicious, angry, extremely secretive, obsessive, and vindictive.

THINK: Prince Charles, Leonardo DiCaprio, Ryan Gosling, Matthew McConaughey, Gerard Butler, Josh Duhamel, Mark Ruffalo

Sagittarius

November 22 – December 21 | Ruled by Jupiter | "~Wanderlust~"

Women: Sagittarius women are probably as iconic in the entertainment industry as Leo women are (two words: BRITNEY. SPEARS.). They love to be the life of the party and enjoy large groups. The difference is that they don't need all the attention. Sagittarians need freedom to roam, to explore, and to discover. They are the philosophers of the zodiac. Nothing makes them happier than debating religious, political, and spiritual topics, and educating the people around them. Sagittarius women are known to expand their friends' horizons, and they get off on changing people's worldviews.

Female Sagittarians are very open-minded, confident, and optimistic. These women hate living life by a schedule or being told what to do. They are usually the ones with the most offensive yet hilarious senses of humor. They're incredibly honest, and they expect the same in return. They hate being fake. When dating, they can't stand restraint of any kind; they want a partner in adventure, not a jailer. Clingy people get on their nerves very quickly.

At their best, they are generous, interesting, and honest—they crave adventure and new experiences. At their worst, they are aloof, callous, and refuse to settle down or grow up.

THINK: Britney Spears, Christina Aguilera, Miley Cyrus, Taylor Swift, Nicki Minaj, Chrissy Teigen, Sarah Silverman, Tyra Banks

Men: Sagittarius men have a bit of Peter Pan syndrome. They are considered difficult to date because not everyone can handle a guy who just wants to wander around and see the world, and not settle down. These guys are beyond fun to be around, so they usually have a lot of friends and admirers. When in love, they give their all, but they need to be constantly challenged or they will get complacent, bored, and lose interest in their partner. Boredom is the worst thing that can happen to Sagittarius men.

They are drawn to smart, intellectual people who can keep up with them and teach them a thing or two about the world, or be willing to learn from them. Curiosity is another quality they are drawn to. They don't necessarily need materialistic possessions to be happy. A life of adventure and travel will be just fine for them. They are born conquerors, so it's best to play hard to get with these guys and let them win you over by getting creative like only they can be. It sounds like a cliché, but it's true, says my friend who has dated three of them.

At their best, they are faithful, honest, generous, exciting, and eternally optimistic. At their worst, they are stubborn, lazy, noncommittal, and always looking for the next thing.

THINK: Winston Churchill, Brad Pitt, Jay-Z, Jake Gyllenhaal, DJ Khaled, Jonah Hill, Judd Apatow, Russell Wilson, Ian Somerhalder

Breakdown (Sun, Moon, Rising, Venus)

So, if after reading this, you're like, "Um, this is a blatant fabrication of my personality, how dare you?!" Don't fret. Every person is ruled by twelve different signs and planets, so when stalking someone's horoscope to see if you guys are a good match, a sun sign is not enough. The most important things to know in someone's horoscope (for beginners) is a sun sign, moon sign, rising sign (or ascendant), and Venus sign. So, like, a lot of fucking info.

The only way to accurately know these things and get a full picture of a person's entire personality is to know where they were born and their approximate time of birth. This may sound borderline stalker-ish, because it is, but a lot of people do get their charts done for fun, and to get a better understanding of themselves. The accuracy really depends on the time of birth.

A moon sign rules your emotions and feelings, and how you act; a rising sign is how people perceive you (aka your first impression); and a Venus sign shows how you love/act when in love, and how you want to be treated in a relationship. In a man's chart, the Venus sign represents the kind of woman he will fall for. Get those birth times, ladies!

Example: If your sun sign is known to be traditionally submissive, but you're the Samantha of your group, you need to check your moon sign.

There are so many nuances and different parts of astrology that complete the full picture of a person, but it can be fascinating, because if done right, it can tell you a lot more than you might have ever found out. So, if you think these descriptions don't match you or the person you are into, it just means you have stronger influences of signs beyond your sun sign.

You Can't Leave, You're My Only Friend!

(The Friendships and the Social Life)

True friendships are made from loyalty, honesty, and a reputation-tarnishing secret that you can hold against them until the end of time.

You Can't Sit Here

Remember when making a friend was just latching onto anyone who was in your lane of weirdness and riding out teen angst together until college inevitably parted you, but you'll now always have the opportunity to say, "Oh, we've been friends for years!" Of course, you exclude the actual number of years because you're not a sociopath about to reveal that you were alive when dinosaurs roamed.

I mean, like, it seemed easy and somewhat natural, I guess? Now, when you bring a new friend into the fold, your other friends stare at you, eyes bulging, confused at the prospect of an interloper infiltrating their safe space of lunacy, embarrassing antics, and general disconcerting behavior that would make any therapist think twice about prescribing anything. (And instead, maybe reach for the phone to inquire about an actual ward at your nearest mental health facility.)

When I brought someone new to our happy hour, my friends genuinely started texting each other in the group chat, of which I was a part, and fearfully asked the others how to act. Do they smile? Are they allowed to be honest? Would the story from last weekend be a solid "no"? How much is too much?

There are so many intricacies in bringing someone new into the fold, because you never know if that person actually, you know, had a healthy upbringing and will think you and your friends are a bunch of deranged idiots who have no regard for their own well-being. All true things, but you never want to expose your crew to that kind of negative, brutal honesty, so you have to play it safe.

TEAM NO NEW FRIENDS. MY BEST FRIEND AND I ALREADY HAVE PLENTY OF PERSONALITIES BETWEEN THE TWO OF US.

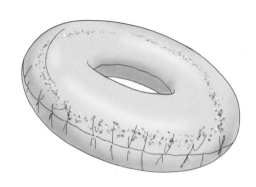

Dip a Toe

We've all heard the phrase about first testing
the waters before jumping right in: you know, dipping the ol' toe.
Although it's one of the least sexy-sounding phrases, it's actually quite true.
Introducing someone new is sort of like that; you need to be conscious
of all your friends, their feelings, and the consequences of what this
spontaneity can do for the friend circle. The politics of female friendships
teach us more about international diplomacy than any UN summit
ever could.

My friend Kelsey once stopped talking to us for a year straight, because
she didn't like that we brought someone random to brunch. That "someone
random" ended up being the girl her soon-to-be boyfriend was hooking up
with for months, before they made it official. Yeah. So, you know, vetting is
definitely something you should do. Plus, in this day and age, it just takes
sending a quick screenshot of someone's Instagram/Facebook/Twitter/
LinkedIn profile to the group chat and you'll know, within five minutes,
whether that person is persona non grata.

So, to adequately gauge
whether you can bring fresh
meat to your lovable, but hostile,
prey, you must first figure this
out: Will they be amenable to it?

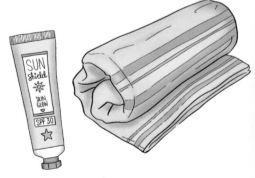

Who Are We?

Society loves to categorize and compartmentalize women, just to keep things "simple," another word they use to describe, and associate with, women. They do so, often, to demean them, reminding them to "know their place." I could delve deeper into this, but this isn't that type of book, so you'll have to settle for my internal outrage. This is all a preface to my introduction of the five types of women I have come to observe, know, and love. Being more of one type of woman doesn't mean you're only allowed to be that; it just makes it a little easier to analyze and have a look at yourself, objectively.

I thought long and hard about how I wanted to describe my friends and me, and introduce the people in our lives, our constant muses, without exposing them too much, along with their trials and tribulations. Each of these categories is based on the very people I interact with daily; that includes learning from them, loving them, and laughing with them. Their mistakes often become my mistakes, and their challenges are ones I know all too well. (I'm talking about *you*, drunk-texting your Chad, just as we all once did.)

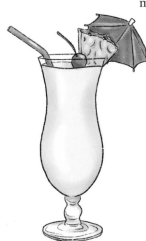

This isn't my harsh microscope on women and all the things wrong with them, but a humorous observation of all the incredible details that come together to make all the strong, amazing, and brave women in our lives. Now, pour a generous amount of tequila and start checking off all the categories you fall into because I am about to throw some truth your way.

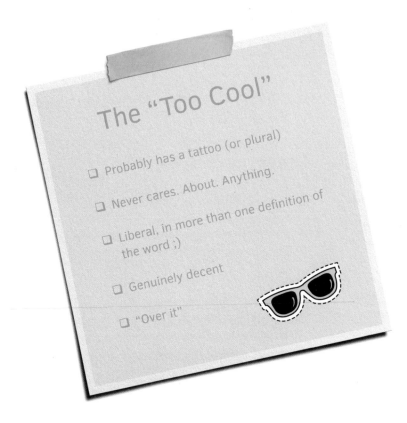

The "Too Cool"

- ☐ Probably has a tattoo (or plural)
- ☐ Never cares. About. Anything.
- ☐ Liberal, in more than one definition of the word ;)
- ☐ Genuinely decent
- ☐ "Over it"

We all know this girl. The girl who, it seems, has it all. She's effortlessly pretty and has that "no makeup" makeup down, because she doesn't stress. About it, or anything else. Her approach to men and life is quite simple: easy come, easy go (literally and figuratively, lol).

She's genuinely just too cool to care, because if it doesn't suit her, it won't last long. Generally, this type of girl has had a solid upbringing and is very independent. She knows herself and is sure of her convictions. She'll try anything once, but only on her terms. And she's a good person, as she's not afflicted with the constant insecurity most girls have, because, from a young age, she was awarded the security that not everyone is fortunate enough to have had.

My life is a constant struggle between trying not to care and simultaneously trying to seem like I don't care.

I'm starting to sound jealous, but again, this is all observational. We could all be this girl on a Friday, technically speaking, but come Monday, when all our decisions settle in, we move past this girl with the lack of grace a truly good hangover provides. I have a friend, Leah, who is this girl to a T, and though it often seems I should harbor a deep amount of anger and jealousy toward her, I don't. (For the most part, sigh.)

She has the strength to be above the pettiness and the games I love to partake in, and she's rather fearless in everything she does. Her decisiveness irks me at times, but only because I try to emulate it, and (shocker!) fail. After her first breakup, with her boyfriend of three years, I thought she would finally succumb to the human qualities *I* know well and love: pettiness and anger. She didn't. I asked her why she wasn't angrier, or hurt, or even slightly vengeful, and she told me, "I still have a lot to be grateful for. He taught me more about myself, and about life, than I would have probably cared to know, and for that, I'm grateful. I now have an experience and a memory I'll cherish forever."

Now you see why I don't hang out with her regularly. That kind of natural wisdom can only be tolerated by a bitter person (like myself) in small doses.

THINK: Serena van der Woodsen in *Gossip Girl*, Kate Hudson in Every. Movie. Ever.

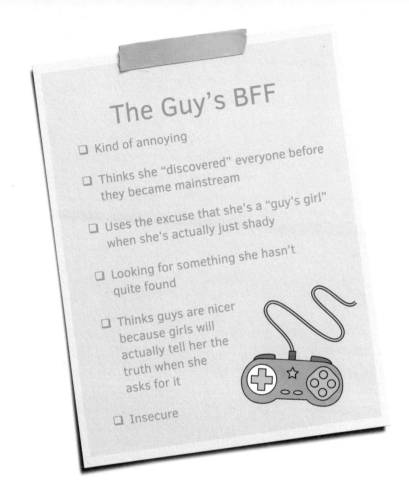

The Guy's BFF

- ❑ Kind of annoying
- ❑ Thinks she "discovered" everyone before they became mainstream
- ❑ Uses the excuse that she's a "guy's girl" when she's actually just shady
- ❑ Looking for something she hasn't quite found
- ❑ Thinks guys are nicer because girls will actually tell her the truth when she asks for it
- ❑ Insecure

This is the girl who will befriend every guy by telling them that girls just usually "hate her" and she doesn't know why. She does. She knows exactly why men are easier to befriend. I don't say this maliciously. I just have too many friends who fall into this category seamlessly, and without fail, will choose a man over a friendship. That's not a criticism, merely an observation.

Men tend to seem more easygoing and less harsh in their judgment of bad decisions, *or so it seems*, and they aren't wired with the attention to detail that women possess. So, if she does something that would be somewhat questionable on the moral-compass scheme of things, it's easier to open up about it to a guy than to a girl, who knows exactly why and how you did it, and knows your steps before you've had a chance to explain your reasoning.

My very good friend Megan (and yes, I am one of her only girlfriends) subscribes to this philosophy. She believes men to be nicer and more accepting, and yet, the second she sees a slightly intimidating woman, in terms of success, looks, or confidence, she becomes hostile and automatically reverts to the offense that this girl "must hate her," setting herself up for a predetermined fate.

She would just prefer to not have the competition of so many women around her, as that would derail the attention away from her, which is something she cannot easily let go of. I often wonder if age will give her the wisdom that validation from men isn't the only thing she should aspire to possess, as she's incredibly smart and talented, but I find myself falling into her trap of "me, me, me," so it would be like the blind leading the blind. We can all relate to my friend because she's just playing into what we all know too well: desire. She wants to feel desire and be desired, and honestly, who doesn't? That's not a flaw; it's human nature. And without getting all existential, it's something out of our control. My friend, and all the women like her, just want to feel loved.

THINK: Demi Moore in the 1980s, Angelina Jolie . . . ALWAYS

This is the girl I always look out for, because, unfortunately, every now and then, this type of girl will find you and you'll believe every sweet word she says. However, as this is coming from a woman, I still stick by her decisions, because who knows what has made her this defensive and insecure? Most likely, it's something incredibly unfortunate and painful, and to fault this girl for acting out is almost selfish.

What I don't approve of, however, is women being unsupportive of one another. There is very little worse than a bad friend, as friendship is all we have in a male-dominated society looking for any crack in the sisterhood. If we, as women, don't come to the aid of other women, we can have very little hope for men doing the same.

Not sure what's more fake: you or the Madonna-esque British accent I develop after three margaritas.

I had a friend, Dana, who was the most doting and loyal friend I could have ever hoped for, but she was also deeply dependent and obsessive. I began to hear of things she was saying about me behind my back, while swearing up and down that others were liars trying to break up our friendship, and I couldn't understand why—why would somebody who so deeply desires my friendship do this?

I found out some years later that she had had a tumultuous upbringing and had been bullied when she was younger, and although that doesn't pardon shady behavior, it also makes it incredibly hard to vilify someone. Her offensive was a defense mechanism from the trauma she had faced in the past (thank you, therapy), which is all too relatable and completely understandable. Her backward approach to relationships, along with her cunning, was the only way she knew how to navigate the waters of life . . . which sounds incredibly profound and deep, but is just kind of sad.

THINK: Every mean girl in a Hilary Duff movie, Gretchen Wieners in *Mean Girls*

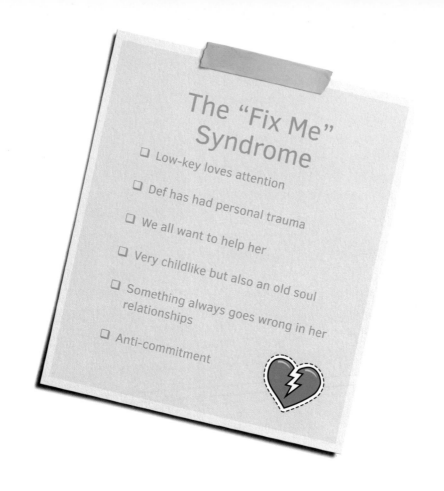

The "Fix Me"
Syndrome

- ☐ Low-key loves attention
- ☐ Def has had personal trauma
- ☐ We all want to help her
- ☐ Very childlike but also an old soul
- ☐ Something always goes wrong in her relationships
- ☐ Anti-commitment

We all know this girl. She's the Manic Pixie Dream Girl from every rom-com ever, here to save your day, all while sacrificing hers. She's everything all the time, and she doesn't know which face to put on each morning. (Zach Braff in the house, yet?) We've all been this girl at one point, yearning and discerning, usually during our formative years when everything is ten times more intense and complicated—every emotion felt with every fiber of our being.

However, in adulthood, this becomes almost terrifying, because what was once cute and interesting has become a genuine problem, and all you

SABOTAGING YOUR OWN LIFE AND THEN EXPECTING EVERYONE TO FEEL SORRY FOR YOU?

Groundbreaking.

want to do is help this person, but nothing you say or do can help. This girl will most likely help those around her; all the while, she herself needs it the most.

Every woman can identify with this archetype, because in each and every one of us, this girl lives and breathes, sacrificing herself for her family, her friends, and her loved ones, and she does so without a trace of hope that there is any compensation, figuratively or literally.

THINK: Effy Stonem in *Skins*, Edie Sedgwick in *Factory Girl* (and life)

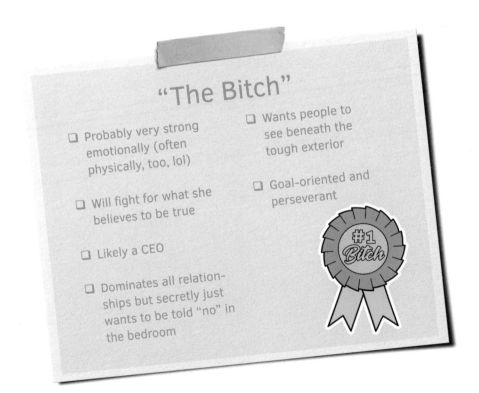

"The Bitch"

❑ Probably very strong emotionally (often physically, too, lol)

❑ Will fight for what she believes to be true

❑ Likely a CEO

❑ Dominates all relationships but secretly just wants to be told "no" in the bedroom

❑ Wants people to see beneath the tough exterior

❑ Goal-oriented and perseverant

#1 Bitch

And finally, we move on to our last, but certainly not least, type—the singular term favored unanimously by all who want to insult a woman and her opinion/independence/prowess: The Bitch.

This is the girl weak men try to avoid, because she's not easily malleable and is far too opinionated. (Probably a future Susan, TBH.) She is someone society will refer to as an outspoken feminist in a derogatory way. She will be the first to defend you, like my dear friend Jen. Jen has constantly proven herself to be a pillar of strength and resilience in a society that almost rejoices in watching women fail when they try, and try, and try, stopping only when they've reached above and beyond their goals.

Jen has never taken no for an answer and continues to impress me with her constant care and friendship, amid all the intensity she has going on in her life. I try, time and time again, to emulate her work ethic and genuine zest for life but always come up short in, well, almost every way, because I love to sleep and my phone is my bestie.

Jen's approach to relationships has always been that if her partner is not contributing, he's taking away. There's no middle ground. And I so deeply appreciate that about her, because it sounds so simple, but it's so inherently true. Why be with somebody who drains you of your strength, or who just doesn't provide anything of substance or value to your already exciting life? And I agree with this for women too. When both parties are bringing something to the table, they will have a respect and admiration for each other that will help build a strong foundation for a meaningful and long-lasting relationship.

THINK: Emma in *No Strings Attached*, Margaret Thatcher in *The Iron Lady* (and life), Paris Geller in *Gilmore Girls*

Now, my therapist is convinced that people will criticize me for writing this chapter that compartmentalizes women into categories, the very antithesis of feminism, a term I use proudly (see page 115).

I apologize if you feel this way, for that is in no way my intention. These are the eyes that I have observed society to perceive women with, and I wanted to clear up the misconceptions in those perceptions, in my own voice.

We live side by side with these women, we know their strengths and weaknesses, and we know, more than anyone, that they constantly fight battles, both internally and externally. By vocalizing these categories, I want them to know they are not alone in their strife and that we have all been one of these women, at one point or another. That's not even remotely a negative thing because each of these categories has its own incredible qualities that make women the backbone of society and the amazing mothers raising the future generations.

Once you've identified which of your friends falls into which category, you can go into the trenches, armed and prepared, for the potential shitstorm that could ensue. I may be using a lot of aggressive analogies here, but, you know, if it walks like a duck . . .

Why Are You Talking to Me?

Dear MTS,

I recently made a new friend, and it feels as though we've known each other for forever. It may sound weird, but we're very similar. I know my best friends would also really like her, but they're not exactly acting thrilled at the idea of my having made another close friend. How can I introduce someone who I think could be a great addition to our friend group without alienating my best friends?

—Laura

Look, it's always fun to add more interesting and exciting people to your already existing group of friends, as long as the balance remains the same and everyone is in agreement. It's kind of tough for a group of friends to all get on board without one person having an opinion that opposes this new addition. If this doesn't happen immediately, the time will come, and someone will have something snarky to say (not being cynical, just experienced).

Personally, some of my current girlfriends, whom I would consider somewhere between best friends and close friends, are recent additions to my friend group. It's not our fault we met later in our lives, and have years to catch up on, but the feeling of closeness, and solidarity, is still there. That kind of chemistry can't be faked.

It's incredibly inconvenient to force yourself to befriend someone and pretend to care about what they have to say. Like, at least if you do this with a guy, you might get a kiss or something out of it. Here? All you're going to get is a headache, impatient, and anger issues. So, if you *do* happen to find someone who shares your love of bad chick flicks, sour cream and onion chips, and *The Simple Life*, and has the opposite taste in men? Lock that shit down! I mean, do so with the consideration of your friends' feelings in mind, but don't let that kind of love pass you by. It's not every day you meet someone else who believes discussing celebrity engagements is, in fact, "current events."

OH, YOU ALSO HATE EVERYONE?

Did we just become best friends?

You Are Who You're With

Which brings me to my favorite point: you are inherently who you associate with. I don't care that you say, "Jenna's a party girl, but we love her!" or "Bailey's a bit too friendly with the vodka sods at every party, but she's still a hoot." If you're truly close with these people, a part of you is internally aligned with something within them.

There's a reason you're close friends, so you now have to start looking at yourself the way people are looking at you when you're with your friends. Are you happy with the way you're being perceived? Having been made aware of the fact that not only are you being judged for who you are, but also for who your nearest and dearest are, does it make you think twice about who you're fraternizing with?

 My Therapist Says that this is all coming out a bit too intensely, but she does agree that we absolutely do look to our friends to get a better sense of who we are. She also wants me to stop casually peppering some of the lingo I've picked up from World War II documentaries into my daily vernacular. ·

Nearing a certain age, as morbid as that sounds, we need to start becoming more aware of who we are and how we want to be regarded. If our relationships relay to others what we hate about ourselves, lol, then what do our friendships say? That was kind of a joke, but our friendships certainly tell people what we find affinity with.

I'm not saying to clean house and dump the posse, but take a look at who comprises the circle of trust you call besties. Your future boyfriend? He's definitely going to be looking as closely at your friends as much as he is at you, if he truly wants to pursue a relationship with you. Your prospective employer? Without a doubt they will not only check your background, but also how you carry yourself outside of the workplace, and with whom. Even your family will pass judgment on who you're inviting over. Although my family can't stand almost all my friends, so who am I to advise?

My Therapist Says no one. You absolutely should not be advising.

As I was saying, there will be haters, but, like Justin Bieber, we all just need to find #Purpose. Nobody wants to be misrepresented, especially in this day and age, when literally everything and anything is acknowledged, represented, and somewhat respected. So, if you're putting in hard work to be taken seriously, at whatever you've chosen to do with your life, it would be incredibly annoying for that to go to hell when people meet your partner in crime, Jessica, who's a stage 10 socio with daddy issues. Just saying.

You can imagine that my therapist was horrified to read that last statement because joking about "socios" is against everything we (she and I) stand for, so she is verbally admonishing me, and she'd like me to document it so you can feel her wrath and disapproval.

My Friend Is Friends with the DJ (or When You Actually Want to Go Out but Are Lazy)

On the rare occasion in which some strange plan strikes your fancy, you decide that it's time to dust off the ol' heels, replace the blanket with a minidress, and take that shower you've been putting off for a few days. Maybe it won't be so bad this time? (how sweet)

I typically find the best course of action in motivating myself to go out involves tequila, loud music blaring from my speakers, and some mascara, to put things in perspective. Netflix and your bed aren't going anywhere, so fear not, fellow introvert. While the horrific Coronavirus quarantine for most seems stifling, claustrophobic, even panic-inducing, for an introvert like me, it's another Sunday in the books. So, if I've made up my mind about actually leaving my house for the purpose of socializing and, gulp, having fun? I am defs committing to it.

If you've already gotten as far as planning what you're going to wear for your night out, you might as well make yourself a drink, and pour it up, honey, because nowhere in this picture are you staying in. And that's not entirely a bad thing. Going out with your friends should be something to look forward to: having fun, letting loose (unless you're like my friend Mal, who could afford to keep it tight every now and again).

My therapist just sighed loudly. That's all.

Anyway, a lot of the anxiety about leaving your home and heading out into the unknown is really just that: it is unknown. A lot of us, myself included, tend to prefer the tried and true. It's honestly why some people stay in a dead-end job, or relationship, or fill-in-the-blank situation, because the thought of breaking out and trying something new terrifies us to the point of refusing to try it before we've even decided to.

So, in this situation, I believe a little "leap of faith" is needed. It might suck. The night might be a complete waste of your time, but breaking habit and trying something out of your comfort zone is sometimes what you need to push you into possibly making one of the best decisions. Often, it's the nights we least expect, or the places we least want to be, that end up changing our lives in the best way possible.

Dear God, I just sounded so New Agey that I talked myself out of ever leaving my house again. K, thanks.

 My Therapist Says this is great advice in building a "new normal" and experiencing things out of our comfort zones, thereby teaching us new lessons and giving us new experiences. Our experiences will shape us and teach us more things, changing our decisions and outlook on life. At the same time, she says it's completely all right to feel uneasy when deciding whether you want to venture out or not, as everyone should take the steps in their own time.

On that note, I'm going to go do something potentially destructive because she just AGREED WITH ME!?!

The 5 Types of People
You Meet at a Party
(aka Reasons Why I Drink)

THE CHAD, BRAD, OR VERY SAD: The namesake for this one comes from a "Chad," a "Brad," or someone who's "Very Sad," just coming off a breakup or dealing with some bad news. This is the person who is the drunkest one at the party, before midnight. They won't shut up about anything and everything, slurring to anyone who so much as pauses too long next to them, so beware. Any small piece of information that's otherwise stupid and unnecessary? Yep, they'll tell you about it. They probably reek of whatever alcohol they've been consuming that night, and feel the need to brag about something that has no importance to them, or anyone, for that matter.

THE MICHAEL SCOTT: This one is inspired by one of the most ridiculous and awkward characters in TV history. This person is both strange and uncomfortable, and you know this because they make *you* feel that way, too. Whether it's discussing something taboo and inappropriate, or accidentally divulging someone's secret, this person makes sure to kill the vibe of any setting. Though not always intentional, or mean-spirited, this person just doesn't know how to behave in crowded settings. Or any settings, for that matter. They're likely this way because of a shortage of friends, and the shortage is likely because they're this way, so . . . don't stand too close.

100% TEARS of MY ENEMIES

THE "I JUST GOT BACK FROM TULUM": This one is inspired by that person everyone hates hearing speak, but like a car crash, you just can't look away. They list all their recent expensive purchases, particularly when no one asked, and their voice gets about three times louder upon any mention of cost. Did you want to know where they literally *just* vacationed? No? Well, too bad! Accidentally make eye contact with them and they'll tell you.

THE "I DON'T USUALLY DO THIS": You'll find this person in a corner, or by the bathroom, flirting with their target, getting ready to leave the party and start their own little party elsewhere, with the guest list being pretttty tight. Yep. It's everyone's favorite slutty friend, proudly finding their way at yet another party. It's not *their* fault they're so friendly, okay? People just naturally gravitate toward them. And then gravitate them toward a bedroom. Or a private room. Hey! They don't usually do this, okay?

THE "CAN I GO HOME YET?": About five minutes into the party, this person is talking about the latest Netflix/Hulu/Amazon Prime/Apple TV+/Disney+/HBO Max show they binged from the comfort of their couch, and how they'd much rather be doing that. Then why are you out, CAROL?! These people have momentary FOMO, which actually being at the party kills, because they realize they have the social skills of George Michael Bluth trying to flirt. Like The Michael Scott, these types are awkward, but more so in the unlikable way, as they think their wanting to have stayed home somehow puts them on a pedestal above the partygoers. Word of advice: Don't invite them in the first place, as they will make a point to remind you, constantly, how they wish they could be at home watching *Friends* reruns.

THE ONLY PERSON
I REALLY WANT TO
HANG OUT WITH
AT THE END OF
THE NIGHT IS MY
UBER DRIVER.
FREE THERAPY.

Irish for a Night
(or How to Make the Perfect Exit from a Party)

Though I subscribe to a philosophy skewing closer to drinking so much that I know when it's time to hit the pavement (sometimes a little too literally), your exit strategy might be your most important party trick yet. As a retired self-proclaimed party girl, I am proud to say I've dabbled in almost every exit style possible, accounting for speed, grace, sobriety, heel height, soon-to-be-closing hot-dog stand, and every other specification you can imagine. While some were taken better than others, I can assume that the people I fell asleep on who had to shake me awake and send me packing all knew this was part of my greater, research-oriented purpose.

The rule of thumb is: if a Carol looks like she's starting to "get loose" (her words, not mine), it's time to gracefully peace-the-fuck-out.

Exit Strategy #1: The Trusted Irish

This style, which has a bad rep for being rude and callous, is also the most efficient and least problematic. This method involves you literally making a clean break for it, without a word, to anyone, as stealthily as you possibly can. It should make people wonder whether you were even AT the party in the first place. It saves you from the countless drunken goodbyes in which every one of your friends proclaims their undying love for you as their best friend, a few guys inevitably ask what you're "up to later" (Later WHEN, Chad?!), and someone asks you to share a ride with them.

IDEAL FOR: speed, pain of any kind, too many drinks

Exit Strategy #2: The Grace Kelly

The self-sacrificing Grace Kelly requires you to put on your best Meghan Markle and schmooze-bye your way out of that room. This method takes time, skill, and patience. It is for seasoned drinkers who are not worried about embarrassing themselves when inebriated. It is also for those trying to get a few business cards in there, so the night isn't a total loss. Save this one for business functions and galas.

IDEAL FOR: socializing, making connections, manners (I guess?)

Exit Strategy #3: "Ugh, My Car's Here!"

This strategy somewhat provides you with the urgency and speed of the Trusted Irish without the part of completely ignoring everyone. It's a great way of saying, "Ugh, I'd have loved to say bye to everyone, but my car just mysteriously showed up SO fast! The cruelty. Sigh." This one is great for when you really don't feel like making the final rounds, but have to do a quick run-by of everyone on your way to the door, avoiding any unpleasantness. Save this one for family events, when your aunts start getting nosy and annoying.

IDEAL FOR: speed, too many drinks, pain of any kind, manners

Exit Strategy #4: Leave Before It Begins

It was either Ernest Hemingway or Diana Vreeland who said, "The best time to leave a party is when it's just beginning," and I couldn't have said it better myself. The best parties are the ones you make an appearance at, giving them a little taste of your party-princess self, and then tap out of before any of the real trouble begins and you start blending into the scene. See, a Carol leaves a party last, so take from that what you will.

IDEAL FOR: mysterious exit, avoiding the whole thing without actually avoiding it

I'd Love to Come, but I Don't Want To

It's 2 a.m. on a Thursday night (aka Friday morning), you've had a few drinks to make the other people around you somewhat tolerable, and you've momentarily forgotten that lying in your bed watching Netflix is what you reeeally want to be doing, so, you know, any decision from this point on is regrettable. You're probably assuming I mean drunkenly texting your ex and asking him to pick you up so you guys can "catch up!"

No. Oh, sweet, naive, innocent, reader, NO. The kind of regret I'm referring to here is the heart-pounding, anxiety-inducing, mind-numbing fear that overcomes you when you realize you've agreed to plans that you have absolutely no intention of upholding. Brunch? 10 a.m.? On a SUNDAY? Haaaaa . . . You know, it's actually kind of admirable that you thought this was something you could see yourself doing at that god-awful hour on Sunday, when you know, very well, you'll be deathly hungover, hoping that the only thing you see is a moving vehicle coming directly at you to end your misery. Were the vodka sodas really worth it?

That's a question for another book, but alas. Below, I have drawn out a simple and easy breakdown of how to get out of these horrifying situations we call "catching up with friends," without a) faking your own death, b) getting caught in a lie, and c) actually having to show up at some point.

My Therapist Says that I need to advise you all to skip this part entirely, but, like our weekly sessions in which she tells me what to do, I say, "Moving on!"

Option #1

Call, yes, I said CALL, said friend you made plans with, hoarse-voiced and sounding as ill as you fucking can, because guess what? You just got a case of the casual strep throat. Cough on cue for performance value. This is your one chance to be Sandra Bullock, so don't fail me, Goddammit.

If they don't pick up: Text, and make it long and full of adjectives synonymous with "mucus," "contagious," "coughing," etc. You get the drill. This isn't the time or place to be modest with the hyperbole.

If they offer to come over and drop something off: Thank them profusely for their kindness, even going so far as to sending five to eight crying emojis, but say that the simple act of even moving around (aka leaving your bed) even seems incomprehensible. This one, technically, isn't even a lie for your hungover ass.

Option #2

A family member showed up, *unexpectedly*, visiting from out of town , and you have no choice but to (UGH!) reschedule! You emphasize how annoyed you are, really huffing and puffing about how much of an inconsiderate bitch your family member is, and how cruel fate's hand has been to you today. Focus on how the only thing you really wanted to do was hang out, but what can you do? Family is family.

If you are in a situation with no actual believable family members nearby: Lie about an aunt. It is almost always an annoying aunt, and no one will question you, as she's far enough to be removed from immediate family, but close enough that you have to stay and entertain her. Sorry!

Option #3

Should this dreaded occasion fall on a weekday, rendering the first two excuses somewhat obsolete, use The Susan (see page 88). Almost any excuse can be conjured out of thin air, when blaming The Susan. Ol' Suse has gotten me out of many a pickle, and she doesn't even know how much I owe her. Blame your boss (Susan) for throwing something unexpected at you, out of left field, so much so that you are now left scrambling just to appease this wild animal. Your friend can't really say anything, as almost everyone has their own Susan.

Pro Tip: To really drive Susan's beast-like demeanor home, feel free to call your friend and have someone (preferably with a shrill voice) screeching in the background, blaring orders at you. Sound panicked, if necessary and feeling creative.

If you are unemployed: You can make anyone who is an overall nuisance in your life a Susan and blame your sudden change of plans on them. Just make sure the person you're canceling on has no way of contacting your Susan, or you're screwed.

Option #4

This one, while being the simplest and most selfish, is almost always the most effective. Pretend that your phone broke, turning it off so that the texts show as not delivered. The person, when following up with a confirmation, and upon hearing no word, will assume you canceled and won't bother you. This one is tricky because once you "fix your phone," you're obligated to do double-time and comprise a long, complicated apology for how your phone broke—the technicalities, the process of getting it fixed, the stress—and how you are at your wits' end. Focus on how this RUINED the one thing you were looking forward to (aka seeing said friend). This one will really require commitment to the cause, and a little bit of literary flourish. Channel your inner Tarantino and write a short, cinematic masterpiece.

Thank me laterrrrr . . .

You Should Smile
More (or How to Pretend You're Not a Bitch for All of 5 Seconds)

Have your parents ever commented, after scrolling through your numerous Victoria Beckham–inspired pics, that you look miserable in every photo, and that, just maybe, you should smile? Yeah, me neither . . .

Look, having a RBF (resting bitch face) wasn't a plan, but a destiny. There are occasions where looking like a massive bitch is acceptable, inspired even, but there are moments when every fellow RBFer needs to decide whether smiling, just for a minute, might be more beneficial.

Grandma's funeral? I know you're not showing up there, cheesing for the paparazzi who are the relatives you haven't seen since you were probably born. Meeting your boyfriend's parents? You better bet you're walking in there—with Britney's ten-million-dollar smile in tow—preaching positivity and good values. It's all about knowing your audience, which is a fact my dear friend Mallory has not embraced. The girl pulled out a sly grin to the unsuspecting doctor performing surgery on her sick mother. That whole sentence gave me chills, but, it's all true.

There will be times when your pearly whites will be required to do the necessary begging that you probably don't want to have to do yourself. Practice a look to pull out on the off chance you're required to shake off the gorgeous exterior of your RBF.

As famous RBFer RBG said, "My mother told me to be a lady. And for her, that meant be your own person, be independent." So, you know, be independent, and unique, and all that, unless you need something done that only your angelic smile can get done for you. Being fake nice is also its own sort of independence, *non*?

I'M SORRY FOR WHAT MY FACE SAID WHEN YOU WERE TALKING. I DON'T KNOW HER.

Mom! The Meatloaf!
(The Adulting and the Future)

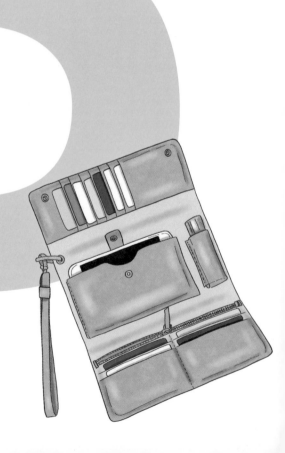

It may look like I'm listening, but I'm really just intently thinking about my next meal.

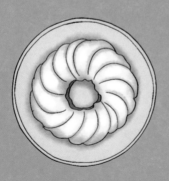

Right?! Am I Right?

Apart from always being right, I have a lot of talents, I think. Listening to people is one of them, mainly because I love knowing that no matter how horribly I think I have it, there's always someone out there, making decisions far worse than mine. In times like those, I make sure to screenshot any receipts I can as proof to show my therapist that I am, in fact, not the bottom of the barrel. But really, for someone as self-absorbed as I am, listening is an attribute I am quite proud of. It could be because I love people opening their wounded hearts to me, looking for my sage guidance, my pearls of wisdom—nuggets I've picked up along the way.

In our modern, and often confusing, times, having an opinion while listening to someone else's and not contradicting it is quite rare. Being a contrarian has become synonymous with being intelligent, somehow. We all know that annoying person who, whenever anyone says something, has to contradict it with their own fact, stat, or Google search, for absolutely no reason other than just because. You can single these people out because they will . . .

a. approach everything with a question, and a follow-up, just so that when they contradict you, and correct you, there will be more impact.

b. listen intently, all while preparing their argument opposing you.

c. lace every word with finely milled condescension.

d. be just as surprised as you are as to why they were invited to the lunch/dinner/party (you can choose whatever the occasion is).

THINK: Both a Carol and a Susan

It's important to have your own opinion, but it's also important to know why you've chosen to have that opinion. If you're going to believe in something, and maybe encourage others to follow suit, then you'd better be informed and understand why. You don't need someone's validation to have an opinion, and you don't always need to be right. It's okay to be wrong, because that just proves that you're willing to learn from your mistakes and keep progressing. Anyone who faults you for your mistakes, and from learning, is just a floser who doesn't need to be in your life, so you'll be killing two birds with one stone.

Similarly, don't force your opinions on others. Nobody wants to be a Susan. You're entitled to believe what you want to believe, and you can encourage and educate others, but after that, build a bridge and move the fuck on.

Learning to differentiate between listening and learning, while not being so malleable that you forget to have your own identity, is an integral part of being that mature, intelligent adult we all strive to emulate. Like, I LISTEN when my therapist advises me not to do something, LEARNING why it will negatively affect me down the line, because I am mature and willing. But I DECIDE to make said bad decision.

I'm, Like, Really Smart Now (or An Easy Guide to Informed Opinions)

1. Try to read up on current events, so that you stay informed of the goings-on in the world and are able to make more informed decisions when discussing said events with your friends/coworkers/randoms.

2. Read books, magazines, newspapers, anything that will broaden your horizons, imagination, and mind.

3. Question things, but not so annoyingly that no one can bear to be around you because you've literally become the antithesis of a fun conversationalist. Unless questioning the thing is integral to your opinion and decision!

4. Study up on subjects that are of particular interest to you, so when discussing them, you show your varied and in-depth knowledge, and become a source of accuracy for people.

5. Don't be afraid to be wrong. That's part of learning and shows that you're able to make mistakes with grace and humility (or so I hear . . .).

6. Be open to changing beliefs you've made/had from a young age. Just because you've been conditioned a certain way doesn't mean another perspective can't be right.

killing it!

I Don't Know, What Do You Wanna Do?

Have you ever been flooded with a plethora of options in regard to where you want to eat . . . six hours after your boyfriend asked you that exact question, lying in bed, wondering why none of those suggestions popped into your head when they were, you know, actually useful? Yeah, me neither.

Why is it that whenever we need to make a decision, we hesitate, overthinking and overanalyzing, even something as simple as where to eat? A lot of criticism aimed at women that I've read over the years seems to consistently talk about our lack of quick decision-making. Powerful men, you see, tend to be "quick on their feet" and "take charge immediately" upon any sudden situation arising. I mean, or so I've read. If I look back at the decisions my boyfriends-past have made, well, I would be doing a disservice to men everywhere. But, it did get me thinking. We do try to see every side of a situation before fully committing to something, because as women, we are analytical. And that's a great thing, but it also makes us really fucking annoying to be around sometimes.

Like, group me with any four friends of mine, and it will take us more time to collectively decide which party to go to than the amount of time we actually will spend at said party. We go through our pros and cons, analyze what the venue will be like, question whether our outfits will be appropriate, estimate what the male-female ratio will be, ponder whether the drinks will be good, and so on—it NEVER ends. Come to think of it, after having spent the appropriate amount of alone time with myself this past quarantine, I genuinely apologize to anyone who's had to do this with me in the romantic sense.

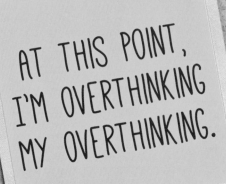

Making quick, assertive moves is something of a skill, really. A GTD*
shows that you're quick on your feet and easygoing, but at the same time,
you know what you want and don't fuck around, all of which are admirable
traits for anyone, male or female. If your boss asks you in a meeting what
you think of the suggestion your coworker just pitched, you're not going to
sit there and say, "Well, um, I need to digest this and weigh the options."
While that's great down-the-line thinking that will help you with an end
goal, it's not the fast-paced, take-charge energy that your boss wants to see
from you. You've got to be assertive, and prove, with the speed of a blink,
that you're always ready.

*GTD: Game-Time Decision

I mean, this obviously doesn't apply to when someone asks you what
movie you want to watch, but you get the urgency. A person with slow
reflexes only showcases to other people that they are of a weaker meld and
not a leader. And like when almost every boyfriend of mine has said that I
am a calming presence, I don't agree. Being slow is being slow. Sure, you're
going to lose a few here and there, but in the grand scheme of things, you'll
be known as somebody who knows what they want.

My Therapist Says that, although it's great to
be proactive and a quick thinker, often taking your time to
make the right and informed decision is a better approach
than jumping the gun too hastily. That approach could
cost you more down the line, whereas five more minutes
of thought might have saved you.

Okay, *that* coming from the woman who consistently says "no," before
I even get a chance to begin the tales of my adventures upon entering her
office? I think the fuck not.

4 Ways to Buy Yourself a Few Minutes of Clarity

1. Nod while looking contemplative, furrowing your brow for effect. Bite your lip, and really look like you're giving it thought, especially if you're drawing a complete blank. **Tip:** When you finally have an answer, but you're not feeling too confident about it, sigh deeply, as though this was a tough cookie to crack.

2. When you immediately know that you have absolutely zero ideas or thoughts on the matter, look the person addressing you in the eye, fully serious and zoned in, and ask them to repeat the question, as though you can't believe that actually just left their mouth. Feign a bit of disdain—make it subtle, and calculated, so even they start to question whether they want you to answer their silly query.

3. If it's a superior, and you want to be agreeable but not a kiss-ass, almost always agree/say yes, but add some sort of suggestion to it, to make it seem like you're both a contrarian and it was your idea, and that everything they think of, you manage, with your enthusiasm and skill, to make a little bit better. Basically taking credit with a slight adjustment.

4. This one is for the truly desperate, but excusing yourself to use the restroom is always an excellent way to give yourself the minutes you need to get it together. It'll also brand you the person who can't hold it in, even to answer one simple question. But when you gotta go, you gotta go.

 My Therapist Says these are in no way helpful, so to each their own.

Be the Ronaldo of Your Life

Whenever I watch *Legally Blonde*, or any Hilary Duff movie ever made, I often say to myself, "This is it! Starting today, I'm going to make goals, and achieve them all, one by one." Of course, come tomorrow, I have amnesia and go back to doing absolutely nothing (except on those rare occasions when I go out, in which case, that's a whole day's prep, but that's for another chapter). Whenever I find myself really motivated after a movie, I get these Napoleonic ideas, which I never really see realized, but I know they're there, hiding in the depths of my laziness and uselessness, clouded by the "maybe tomorrow"s and the "I can't do EVERYTHING, can I?"s.

The importance of setting goals and writing them down is that seeing something written down, in bold ink, will continually remind you of your quest toward greatness, making it somewhat permanent. It also makes your reluctance and laziness in pursuing these goals less of a hindrance and more of a small hurdle. Goals are what we have in our heads to keep us going, knowing there is a brighter light ahead.

Again, not everyone reaches every goal, but not every goal is too great to reach. Winning-an-Olympic-medal goal to one person is a writing-a-short-story goal to another. We all have different goals that we'd like to see realized, no matter how big or small, but it's the act of actualizing them that seems to escape most of us. We can, honestly, sometimes work years toward our goals, but they're our very own green lights. For Gatsby, his goal, all those years, through all the challenges, and trials, was Daisy. He went years in a silent pursuit, dominating one field to the next, throwing soiree after extravagant soiree, all to see his dream of finally being reunited with Daisy realized. *That* is a long-term game plan.

If You Love Me, Let Me Go

I used to date this incredibly delusional, toxic person whom I was convinced I was in love with. It didn't matter how many times we broke up, and made up, only for it to happen again (see The Cycle on page 78), but this time with a touch of flair for dramatic effect, so we never got too boring for our unwilling audience (our friends). What mattered was that I was on autopilot making these decisions, living each day as though I just knew what the next one would bring, in terms of this unhealthy cycle, but also completely in the dark of how much worse it would get, until, one day, I made an active decision to pick myself up and move the fuck on. That sounds really easy in theory, but it took eight months to actually do it, and force myself, day by day, to make the conscious decision to not revert back to my old ways, to not fall back into the cycle that ultimately ends the same way. That wasn't just a GTD (see page 195), it was a LTG*.

*LTG: Long-Term Goal

Sure, there were moments, post-tequila and late-night karaoke, when I almost faltered and wanted to make a very poor GTD, but I never did. Not once. Because like someone rehabilitating from a painful addiction, I felt the sweet taste of the freedom of not being chained to the darkness. My God, I just got real Enya there for a minute.

Even my therapist was convinced I'd crack after a few margaritas, but—if only to stick it to her and lord it over her for the rest of my life—I never allowed myself that weakness. It's exhilarating how powerful you feel when you want to prove someone wrong. Like, when my therapist once said I couldn't (or was it shouldn't?) make the same mistakes year after year? Got her there, too!!!

Making long-term decisions that will affect you more permanently is just as important as making decisions to get you out of momentary discomfort, but LTGs are def decisions you should devote more than two seconds of thought to. They'll be decisions that determine the fate of your relationship. Or your career prospects. (Or your deep-seated daddy issues.) But tough, everyday decisions they will be. And the only way to conquer them is with adequate grace and humility, two adjectives I myself have come to be known for. Or so I tell myself, on day three of a bender. There are three rules I live by when making grand decisions, that will probably screw me over:

1. Think it over, from every angle. There is no overthinking here, because the more you think, the better. It'll only benefit you. The more perspectives you can see it from, the clearer the picture will become.

2. Look at the impact this goal may have on you. Will it lead you upward, or will it tear you down? Never forget that after you've made your bed, you'll be the one lying in it. You want Egyptian cotton, NOT polyester blend. Ugh.

3. Feel it out. What types of feelings is your goal bringing out in you? What you feel matters most, because it'll affect your state of being. You can't be sipping rosé on a rooftop while feeling bummed out!

Once you've figured it out, with honesty and clarity, you can go ahead and make the decision.

My therapist is beaming with pride at this advice, cheesing ear to ear like an overfed chipmunk (there's a sight I could've gone without seeing).

The thing with not achieving your goals is there's always some obstacle, mythical or not. You may not have the opportunity, which is fair. If your goal is to be a tennis player and you can't afford a racquet, let alone lessons, something like that really *is* out of your control. But, looking at it from the other side, you can say, "Okay, I can't afford it now, but I'll get a job, save up, and I won't allow anything to stop me from pursuing this. Once I become good enough, I can get a scholarship." To avoid sounding too *The Secret*-y, what you're doing is changing the narrative. And sometimes, that helps.

In particularly glum situations, changing the narrative and looking at something from a completely different point of view, while delusional, can also help you momentarily forget about your dire situation. While this may sound like I'm advocating for you to temporarily lie to yourself, it's because I am.

pause as my therapist inhales a long, deep breath—she suspects where this is headed, I'm sure

I advocate for a lot of things I don't follow through with, which is why there's that adage "do as I say, not as I do." Seriously, spend a day in my shoes and you'll never want to own shoes again. However, I do believe that telling yourself whatever is necessary in the moment, to get yourself to where you need to be mentally to achieve your goal, isn't a crime. It's a mode of operation. Like, realistically, was Elle Woods really Harvard material? On paper? No, probably not, but it was due more so to her belief that she was better than that. And that's the moral of that story: *she* was too good for Harvard, but slummed it for a second to get her boyfriend back, only to realize, um, she can do *better*! Be like Elle Woods.

On the following pages, write down every long-term goal (it may only be one) you would like to see realized, within the next five years. Think of where you'd want your archnemesis to bump into you, looking chic and fabulous, with your dream job/body/relationship/life. Don't be shy.

Now, if you ever feel yourself losing steam, just place your enemy in your position, with your dream job, body, relationship, and life, and wake the fuck up because you would sooner burn this book to ashes than see that happen. Stay motivated! And if you're still finding it hard to stick to your goals, even after you've reread your reasons for wanting to achieve them, then let's mosey on over to the checklist (see page 207) that you DON'T want to score high on. If you can check off two or more of those, ABORT MISSION.

LONG-TERM GOALS
(or I'll Probably Regret
This Later)

*Write down the goals that you would like to track
between now and the next five years, or whatever.*

Goal #1

Goal #2

Goal #3

Goal #4

Goal #5

The It's Not My Goal, It's Me Checklist

❑ You may be, and very well are, drunk—tequila, wine, vodka, I don't care.

❑ You're emotional: that time of the month, alcohol, loneliness, bad day, take your pick. If you're driven by momentary loneliness because "something happened that day," this is not it.

❑ You got into a fight with your friend/coworker/boyfriend/family member. Nope, still not a good enough reason.

❑ Your friend got engaged.

❑ You were fired from your job.

❑ Your friend told you that it's fine, but she's also drunk. **Tip:** If your friend told you it's fine and she's NOT drunk, she's probably not your friend.

❑ You think it'll be "funny." Liar. No you don't.

And if after that, you still can't stick to it or abandon it completely? Well, in that case, I'll just pour one out for you now, pal, because you are SINKING in my ship, and misery loves company.

So, the World *Doesn't* Revolve around Me?

So, you've exercised literally every ounce of strength and brainpower that you possess and you're still no closer to going from Rachel Markle to Meghan, Duchess of Sussex. You still don't have unlimited access to Bergdorf's, and the closest thing you have to a relationship is your Uber Eats app, checking in on you daily, feeding you, and providing different codes as a little treat every now and again. That's okay. You're fine. No need to bust out the sage just yet.

I know better than anyone how one person can try their absolute hardest, put all their strength and belief into something, and utilize every option available to them, and still, their therapist *will not* pick up. While it's important to be headstrong, ambitious, and determined, it's also important to be aware that things may just be out of your control, no matter your effort or willingness. There will be moments where it feels as though the world is against you. That's okay. Take those days as days of respite from your enviable worker-bee prowess and distract yourself with something else entirely, so your mind isn't focusing on the glaring hole left by your lack of goal-getting.

You'll be okay. Those storms will pass, a new dawn will break, and a fresh day will start for you to conquer new challenges on the way to achieving your dreams. No success story is complete without experiencing these kinds of intricacies. Say your goal was to be engaged by a certain age, yet a certain boyfriend wasn't stepping up to the plate? Well, instead of having him hypnotized into proposing against his will, take some time instead to really think about the situation: Is he really the one, and is this really the path you want to stay on? Maybe there is some greater

Surprise, Surprise . . .

My Life Is Going to Shit

Again: A Memoir

purpose to his stalling, freeing you up for some other opportunity. A newer model, perhaps?

My therapist didn't approve of that one.

An opportunist, the best kind of person, in my opinion, manages to find the silver lining of opportunity in every situation, no matter the circumstances. I mean, I'm sure funerals are a no-go zone, but other than that, it's a free-for-all.

Aaaaaand there goes my therapist, out the door.

Moving on. When you see a clear path, and suddenly, it becomes covered with piles of unnecessary shit, and you still try to prevail, even through the foul odors and the glaring signs, until finally you realize you need to stop trying to find the clear path, but look instead at all the stuff around it? Why has it suddenly become so impenetrable? Most of the time, I try to be reasonable, and barrel through, even when unwanted—*especially* when uninvited. But when the moment cometh, when even I feel a chill in the air and a tickle in my throat, I decide it's best to tread lightly, and perhaps, move the fuck along.

Overcoming obstacles is one of the lessons you always hear about, on the climb to greatness. Greek philosophers waxed poetic about it, romanticizing the hard labor that goes into achieving a measly dream. And, while admirable and certainly necessary in some instances, it really is just screaming at you that maybe this isn't your road, and to take the hint and find another one? Robert Frost said there were two, *non*?

It sounds particularly unfair and hard to randomly change course, because of some unprecedented change to your existence that suddenly jolts you alert to how life doesn't always play to your finely tuned melody, but such is the process. You could be moments away from tasting the sweet and rewarding fruits of your labor—victory, at last—and just as suddenly, one phone call could change the course of your life forever. These are the obstacles you must prepare yourself for—not the small losses you'll endure, but the big ones for which you'll have no answer and no respite, but an utter helplessness overcoming you. It is in that moment that you must pick yourself up and continue through. Did Gracie Hart stay down when she fell on the stage in the Miss United States pageant? I think the fuck not. If you want to become Miss Congeniality, get up and keep going.

And learning to differentiate between the fight or flight (to a completely new path) moments will be the true testament of your strength yet. Personally? I've chosen flight into the safe and (almost never) loving embrace of my trusted therapist too often. Ultimately, in this unpredictable course of life, you're going to have highs and lows, both of which you will learn valuable lessons from (hopefully), and unlike me, actually take those lessons and utilize them into creating a better future for yourself. I've seen this happen to many a friend—whether it was an unforeseen breakup or a job loss—almost consistently, without fail, ending up being a blessing in disguise. Blessing for which party is debatable, but somewhere in there, in the failure and despair, a blessing there was.

Love That for Us!
(The Insecurities and the Self-Care)

My confidence goes from Beyoncé at the Super Bowl to actual potato within seconds.

A 7 with Beer Goggles

A lot of the questions my therapist and I answered for you throughout this book had an underlying insecurity about them, like "What would so-and-so think if I did this?" or "How can I change myself to be more like this person?" Everyone gets insecure. If you don't have insecurities, then you're just as delusional as I am.

So, what can be done to conquer your insecurities? I am an ardent believer that your insecurities are ruining your life. You must combat and silence them. I am also never leaving my house without makeup on, so do as I say and not as I do.

If your bestie had a date and you went over to her place to pregame and help her get ready, and all of a sudden she breaks down crying, screaming about her every flaw, would you calm her down, telling her that, although everyone has flaws, those flaws are what make them human and unique? Or would you tell your bestie to shut the fuck up, get hot, and go out on her date, because she's an all-around 10 in your eyes?

My friends and I have had many a mental breakdown pre-party and pre-date, somewhat composing ourselves just seconds before our arrival was expected. Insecurity is a beast that strikes at the least opportune moments, getting into your head and opening your eyes to every imperfection, magnifying them so much so that they become the

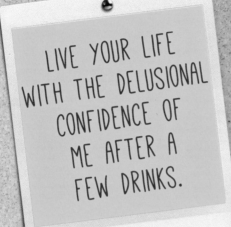

LIVE YOUR LIFE
WITH THE DELUSIONAL
CONFIDENCE OF
ME AFTER A
FEW DRINKS.

only thing you see each time you look at yourself. The great part about beauty, though, is that it is subjective, like when you and your friend can't agree on a guy whom you both find attractive, because she likes blonds and you favor brunettes. It really is that simple. What is beautiful to one person may not be the other person's style, so it's important to remember this, and to remind yourself and your friends, on your darkest of days, that everyone's perspective is unique and different, and that doesn't take away from their beauty.

Ever since we were incredibly young, and learning to be conscious of our appearance, a multitude of avenues appeared to us, telling us to straighten our hair, use mascara, befriend concealer, lose ten pounds, and so on. The goal was always to aspire to be more—be more beautiful, be more intimidating, be more confident, and just, in its simplest definition, be more. While it's great to set goals, and achieve them for YOUR happiness, finding flaws in your appearance, and changing how you look because of them or because someone else tells you so, is where the water becomes murky. It seems ridiculous to even try, if you think about it, to be "perfect" because that can mean so many different things.

It's okay to be insecure, but the difference is learning to draw a line between letting that insecurity consume you and letting it strengthen you and moving away from it.

My therapist just visibly paled. Even she's shocked at my sound wisdom.

dusts shoulders off In all honesty, though, everyone is afflicted with the turmoil of insecurity. It varies, sure, but it's there, and that's fine, as long as it doesn't dictate your life. You can think and feel a certain way that maybe isn't the most conducive path to finding success, but let your actions be led by your bravery amid the insecurity. Eventually, when it settles in how much you're capable of when you're not second-guessing yourself, everything else will fall into place.

It's like Shonda Rhimes's book, *Year of Yes*, I think. Having never actually read the book, it sounds like I'm on the right track: saying yes and going for it, even when fear may lead you elsewhere. Fear is the foundation of insecurity. Resisting the urge to fall prey to your fears, you can begin the process of combating insecurity.

Those words came from the mouth of my therapist, but I was thinking them.

And when all else fails, remember this: Kim Kardashian started organizing closets for Paris Hilton, and look at the two of them now. Sure, there's been a sex tape or two along the way, but that's more of a personal choice. The moral of the story is, it's not where you begin, but where you end up.

do it FOR yourself

Ugh, I Got So Fat

You know when you're looking in a mirror and you realize how genuinely grossed out by yourself you are, at least for that moment for absolutely no reason? Then, your mother calls, and asks you the same thing you've been thinking as you look into that mirror: "Did you gain weight?" You then tell her to leave you alone, hang up furiously, and blame everything wrong in your life on your mother. There goes years and years of therapy . . .

Why is it okay for us to think a certain way about ourselves, but when someone verbalizes our thoughts to us, we start to resent them and think they're mean? Are they not just saying exactly what we're thinking? If we fault them for criticizing us, why don't we fault ourselves and stop the criticism? Though that sounds incredibly wise and easy to do in theory, it's obviously not quite so simple to execute.

Hating oneself has been around for centuries. Like that philosopher, Blaise Pascal, when talking about Cleopatra, saying, "Had her nose been shorter, the whole face of the world would have been changed." Um, thanks, bro? I'm sure Cleopatra, with all the many things she already had going on in her head, like ruling an empire and stuff, loved that you also thought her nose was a little too long. All of us have things we wish we could change, make better, be better, but hearing it out loud, from others, makes us believe them to be true just a little more, because it's not coming from our insecure heads, but from the mouths of people we consider friends. Or family.

My Therapist Says it's a lot easier to forget a thought like that and move on from it when it's coming from within, because you can compartmentalize it, but when you hear it out loud from someone you respect, it hurts that much more because they are confirming what you had already believed to be true, making it more concrete and harder to escape. This is why it's so important for you to have strong convictions, so when others are all too ready to tear you down, the foundation you've built for yourself withstands the criticism, and takes it in constructively, or shrugs it off.

I, to the shock of literally anyone and everyone, agree with her. If you think you're a baddie, your friend telling you you look like a pumpkin in orange won't bother you, because you'll just think she's jealous. *A sexy gourd, you mean.* Learn to take criticism, if constructive and conducive to making you a better you, positively. And if not constructive? Laugh it off, because you just met yourself a hater, my friend, and you know how we feel about haters.

Love Yourself 'Cause No One Else Will

You're in a meeting, dressed in your finest somewhat-presentable ensemble, feeling particularly fresh and fierce, channeling your inner Tyra, and hoping this is your moment to, in the words of Mariah, "Shine, darling!" You're about to open your mouth, but before any words escape, you mentally black out, your mind now confused, lost, and panicked. Your hopefully soon-to-be boss looks at you expectantly, wondering what the fuck is wrong, and if you can get on with it because they are for-real craving a burrito right about now, and your chances of getting this job are getting slimmer and slimmer. You lick your lips a few times, trying to compartmentalize whatever nonsense you still have left in your head, and regret every decision you've ever made that has led you to this point. You heave a deep sigh, because you know very well that you are colossally fucked.

These kinds of mental lapses tend to happen when people have anxiety, are racked with nerves, or stress, or any of the many things that accompany us in our day-to-day routines. That's why it's so important to have a somewhat stable grasp on your well-being, both mentally and physically, if only to be able to have a better chance at surviving these moments.

It's Anxiety O'Clock

Below is a little list I wrote out to prep myself before any big meeting or presentation, where I know I'll probably mentally black out due to anxiety and stress. I read it over and over until it's ingrained in my brain where, yes, I still black out, but at least now I have something else to focus on:

- Will this matter in five years? If no, chill the fuck out. If yes, well, don't think about that.

- Why are you nervous? Describe it. In detail. Why, or who, or what, is making you feel that way? Once you understand it, you can start to work past it.

- Are you prepared? Well, I hope so, especially if it's something important.

- If you still have the shakes, do something to calm yourself. Whether it's drinking a calming tea or meditating, don't be idle. (Tip: Take half a shot? Just kidding. Maybe.)

- Lie to yourself. Tell yourself you've got this, you're calm, and this is of no importance. You'll be surprised at how your subconscious will pick up on the lie and use it to your advantage.

- If you already know it won't go well, blame everything on a Carol.

- And my favorite tip of all: only a few more hours and it's acceptable to go for a drink!

Eat, Pray, Someone Love Me

I know it seems like the constant lesson I preach, apart from therapy being so great, is to lie, lie, lie, and though that is something I emphatically endorse to benefit you, even with the constant shrieks of horror from my therapist, it's not the fundamental one. Obviously, having faith and trust in the person you're committed to are also important takeaways, if not the most important ones, and I would hope that they go hand in hand. I also hope, for your sake, that this thought is shared by both people in the relationship, because as we've read, and heard, being on the same page is integral to the foundation of a relationship.

Another takeaway is that placing too much of yourself in a relationship is incredibly unhealthy. Like, do you want your wedding portraits to star your husband with a "Featuring You" section? (here's looking at you, Justin Timberlake and Jessica Biel)

You know how you watch Mariah Carey get carried around the stage, like a toddler, from one side to the other, never lacking the true extravagance and indulgence our elusive chanteuse is known for? That's how you should live life. On your terms. So what if society says you're spoiled and demanding? Those are words they use when jealous. I'm sure, over time, Nick Cannon became physically exhausted from having to carry Mariah up and down that winding staircase in her mansion, and exited because he knew he no longer deserved to be around the presence of true and lasting greatness. That's the approach you need to have in your relationships. If you're incapable of finding a celebrity relaysh you can feel affinity for, then are you really even in a relationship?

My therapist is physically fighting my laptop away from me, hoping this never sees the light of day, but alas, the joke is on her . . .

Look, although what I wrote above is heavily exaggerated and punched up for dramatic flair, I stand by it. I want women (and some men) to finish this book and reclaim their right to be self-indulgent and cater to their whims, like men have done for generations. Of course, do everything in moderation, but do what you want, be who you want, and think how you want. Someone who loves you should want you to want the best for yourself, and vice versa. It's not doing things to the detriment of your partner, but doing things that, ultimately, will benefit you both by way of both being happy. You can never be your best in a relationship if you're not your best for yourself first.

The Balancing Act

You're juggling, say, a family, maintaining the romance in your relationship, actively pursuing a promotion at work, and balancing your friendships and social life, all while trying to be healthy and implement some sort of workout into your day; it is *a lot*. A lot of everything. So, how do you manage it all?

1. **You must always prioritize yourself, because if you're being overlooked, it could all come crashing down.** You are the key piece to the intricate puzzle that is your life. It is with an unnerving sense of annoyance that we watch how women have to "balance it all," and the one who does it the best is rewarded, whereas the ones who are doing *their* best get overlooked for being seemingly not enough. You can't be expected to be a pillar for others when made of sand. I know. That was really poetic.

My therapist kind of did a double take after that one.

2. **Second, you have to learn how to prioritize and extricate yourself from situations that aren't working for you.** Women are known to take on so many things, saying yes to everything (whether they don't want to seem ungrateful or for whatever reason), without considering the repercussions. Those repercussions could end up being a breaking point, so you have to find a rhythm that works for you and ride that tide. Everyone is different, and if it seems like you aren't doing as much as the mother next to you, or your friend who just got promoted, or even your sibling who seems like she has it all together, that's okay. Do things at your pace so the longevity is there. You can try to do something quickly, and then crash and burn, or you can be meticulous and patient, seeing it through to the successful end, minding your time, sanity, and well-being.

3. **Don't be fearful.** Women are cautious because we've been taught from a young age to be careful because we're delicate beings, unlike, you know, the big, burly men. We lead with that fear in almost everything we pursue. That fear will dictate whether you stand up for yourself in a difficult situation, it will dictate whether you ask for a well-deserved raise, and it will even dictate how you approach your relationships. Being mindful and cautious are great qualities, but at certain times, they can hinder progress because you're overanalyzing everything for fear that you're letting recklessness steer you. This is a barrier many women face. Because of certain circumstances, sure, women do need to have a healthy amount of caution when pursuing certain avenues, but that doesn't mean that they can't adopt the assertiveness and fervor that is not only encouraged, but embraced, in men. Even with the fear and hesitation, take the leaps you think are too big and climb higher than you've been conditioned to believe you're meant to go, because, often, those leaps of faith are rewarded in miraculous ways.

The Therapy

Nearing the end of our journey together, I can only impart so much more wisdom on you before you outgrow even my sage guidance and valuable advice. This advice that I've so generously passed on, I've learned in therapy. Therapy is something I talk a great deal about, and is something I've devoted a part of my life to. For me, it was something I needed to face adulthood and the responsibilities that accompany it.

But therapy is also many other things: a place where I can literally go on and on about myself and my therapist has to just sit there and pretend she doesn't want to immediately toss a Xanax down my throat. It's a tranquil oasis where, for an hour and half of my salary, I feel momentarily at ease. A haven where I concoct strategies to better channel my anxiety so it doesn't overtake my life in a way that it is completely out of my control. So, therapy, you can say, is something I do for my mental health.

I find mental illness to be fascinating, because so many people go about their days without knowing what exactly is happening with them, but feeling like they just don't fit in. Mental illness continues to be portrayed by some as though every person who has any relation to it should be in a straitjacket getting lobotomized, but those times are far behind us, fortunately. We've advanced so far with our technology, our society, even our beliefs, and yet, we still approach mental illness in the cautious, taboo fashion that we reserve for herpes. Okay, that joke was in poor form, but you get what I'm trying to say.

Does This Have Gluten?

Ideally, I would follow this up with what I do for my physical health, like a few Peloton sessions, or yoga, for the full-body experience, but that, like every admission of mine thus far, would probably be a lie. However, I'm all for the complete package: a healthy body and a healthy mind. I've even dabbled in a cleanse here and there, or a variation of one, because, let's be real, I have the willpower of a four-year-old, and I found the results to be troubling . . . troubling because, and I type this with a heavy gulp, they work. Not eating things I know my body is extremely allergic to has helped my mind gain clarity. And not drinking alcohol during the week was the gift my boss never dreamed of seeing realized.

That one week I went to yoga (to prove to my friends that it would do zero for me in terms of advancing my overall well-being) ended up only proving one person wrong: me. To avoid feeling as stupid as I felt that seventh day, after my final yoga class, glowing and proud, heed my advice: find something you enjoy and integrate it into your daily routine.

I'm trying to avoid sounding like the New Age Burning Man Barbie we all love to hate, but I do think that doing something daily—either that you somewhat enjoy but is great for you, or that you love and gives you something to look forward to—could be a great way for you to channel your anxious energy into something useful.

Some people like running, others cycling, and some, like myself, prefer telling others what their preference should be and feeling good about themselves. My friend Jaclyn swears by her one-hour-daily bicycle ride that helps her take out her anger, confusion, aggression, and stress. She is still full of all those things, don't get me wrong, but if she believes it helps her be slightly less annoying, who am I to dissuade her? Find something that you believe in and something you believe can ease some of the burdens you may be carrying, be they metaphoric or literal, and try to pursue it in a somewhat habitual way.

Of course, there are people who have jobs, and families, and aren't fortunate enough to have free time to pursue whatever they please whenever the mood strikes, but even if it is infrequent, you have to do something that prioritizes *you* first and foremost, so you can be the best version of yourself for others. And that is the whole point of caring for yourself, because when you learn to prioritize yourself and love yourself in its full iteration, you'll then consistently attract and only accept that kind of behavior toward you, which is just another added benefit of celebrating your biggest fan: you.

On the right, fill out the timetable for seven days straight, and at the end of day 7, write the difference you've noticed in this week compared to the other weeks when you weren't doing something to benefit yourself.

7-Day Timetable

For the next week, focus on you and write down those little (and big) things you're doing for yourself each day. Are you doing enough? Do you need to do more?

DAY 1

- ☐ _____
- ☐ _____
- ☐ _____
- ☐ _____
- ☐ _____

DAY 2

- ☐ _____
- ☐ _____
- ☐ _____
- ☐ _____
- ☐ _____

DAY 3

- ☐ _____
- ☐ _____
- ☐ _____
- ☐ _____
- ☐ _____

DAY 4

- ☐ _____
- ☐ _____
- ☐ _____
- ☐ _____
- ☐ _____

DAY 5

- ☐ _____
- ☐ _____
- ☐ _____
- ☐ _____
- ☐ _____

DAY 6

- ☐ _____
- ☐ _____
- ☐ _____
- ☐ _____
- ☐ _____

DAY 7

- ☐ _____
- ☐ _____
- ☐ _____
- ☐ _____
- ☐ _____

Famous Last Words
(and Then Some)

It's pretty evident that I don't exactly adhere to the "guidelines" set for me by my (not really) faithful therapist, but the sentiment is there: *I try*. I tried not to hack into my boyfriend's phone, but my hands slipped. The *trying* was there, okay, people! My relationship with my therapist has ebbed and flowed, although she might try to claim that it has been exclusively ebbing. It takes bringing in another perspective to see, through their eyes, how wrong your situation really is, or how many truly God-awful decisions you can make until you realize you are an all-around embarrassment.

We're all guilty of overanalyzing—ourselves, our friends, Britney and Justin's never-going-to-happen reunion. Anything we can analyze, we probably will. It's in our nature as humans to question things, to study them, and to find a reason for why certain things are the way they are. The same can be said for the study of people. Therapists study you, getting to the root of who you are, and start from there. Facing reality, especially right now, can be frightening, overwhelming, and leave you feeling uncertain. Our society, our beliefs, our opinions—they're constantly being questioned, and expanded, toward a positive change, for the most part. It's those moments in between, however, filled with the anxiety of saying, or doing, the wrong thing, when I've found both my mental and physical state drained, and terrified.

Am I putting enough of a conscious effort to combat the stigmas associated with mental health? Am I aware of my privilege and supporting those who are marginalized to the best of my ability? Do I lead with empathy when trying to understand the plight of those who've had to bear a heavier burden than me? It is questions like these, and so many more, that I try to ask myself every day, because I know that as a somewhat fully formed adult (with the few brain cells that I have left), it is not only my duty, but also my responsibility. And while, yes, I have told you that my responsibilities typically include not leaving a drop of Sauvignon Blanc undrunk or a burrito untouched, I have also grown—in the span of writing this book, and in my years in therapy. Yes, plural. *Ugh, whatever.*

All in all, it's safe to say I advocate therapy wholeheartedly. It's shaped me into the person I am today, and the one I hope to become, barring a few little slipups and mishaps along the way. Do I think therapy will answer every great dilemma that's burning on your mind? No. But I do believe that with patience, and belief in yourself, and utilizing your anxious prowess for good rather than self-harm, therapy can help you. Since I'm already getting into my Mia Thermopolis–speech mode, I might as well break it down for you. Talking to someone, from personal experience, can make a world of difference. Hearing out loud the horrors of your mind, or the fears that plague your nights, or the memories that leave with them an awful sensation, can make them as powerless as they once made you. To verbalize your fears, and speak of them, is the first step to releasing their hold over you.

Now that I've inspired you enough to make decisions based on being a decent, thoughtful person, I can go back to the pits of depravity where I comfortably roam. Of course, I have more advice to shower you with; I could go on in volumes, if given the chance. But I won't, so I'll settle for these couple hundred pages of what mostly not to do.

In the words of the prophet Kelly Clarkson, "My life would suck without you." All of you. The ones who wrote in questions, the ones who bared their souls in the form of memes, and my friends and family, who've yet to leave me on the side of a road with very little hope of making it back home. You're the reason I learned that fear is the stupidest thing to have dictate your life, that regret is the most bitter of memories when looking back. I will now never have to ask myself "What if?" . . . since I already showed up at my ex-boyfriend's house unannounced, for the twelfth time, delightfully reading this book to him.

What if you made that call? What if you asked for the promotion you deserved? What if you did everything you wanted to do? This is the part where I break off the tiara into a million little pieces and fling them at you guys to catch.

Will I continue to make the same mistakes I wrote about? Probably. Is winning still the most important thing to me? Only in the eyes of my enemies. BUT, have I learned all the lessons I tried to impart to you? Hard to say. It's not hard to say, however, that if you take anything away from any part of this book, it's that you need to enjoy the life you have, because tomorrow, as we've seen, isn't guaranteed. Our lives are our own, so make your poor choices, laugh at your misfortune, learn to have fun in even the most ridiculous of situations, because when you're looking back on these years later in life, you'll want to be able to say that you did it all, without fear of failure or judgment. Unless you clap when the plane lands, I can't help you there. Make your mark, in the unique fashion you're known for, so you'll never have to ask yourself, "What if?"

Now, excuse me
while I refuse to take
my own advice.

If by morning routine, you mean

_____

until I've had my

_____ ?

Then yes, I have one.

TEXT MY

_____?

AFTER THREE

_____?

DON'T MIND

IF I DO.

My

_____

explains the

amount of therapy

I need.

NO ONE:

ME: _____

_____

_____

_____

A Note about the Text

My Therapist Says . . . Advice You Should Probably (Not) Follow was written in the singular voice of the girl we imagined possessed all the qualities we share, embodying someone our readers and followers could relate to. We combined our humor, our stories, your questions, and our imaginations to create this oracle to guide you through this mystical tornado called life.

Acknowledgments

First and foremost, this book would not have been made possible without the incredible people whom we here at My Therapist Says call family: our followers. Thank you so much for supporting us, believing in us, and sharing with us your stories. Your voices, your honesty, and your kindness keep us going daily, through all the margaritas, exes, and all-nighters. We're all growing together, albeit with little grace and lots of shame, but we would be nothing without you.

Our actual family, who, upon reading this book, may disown us: our Mothers and Fathers. (We love you. We're sorry. We can't.) Our team at Quarto: Erin, Rage, Lydia, and Laura! Thank you for constantly believing in our vision and our (questionable at times) humor. Our grandparents, aunts, uncles, cousins, and distant relations, who've constantly asked us when this book will finally be done: we miss you every day. Max: friend, agent, and confidant. Thank you for being there. But lastly, and not at all in the least, our friends and loved ones: Scott, Dean, Andrew, Johnny, Stacie, Carrie, Paula, Wes, Jess, Allie, Anna, Stevie, Andre, Jenn, Tiane, Tina, Helen, and everyone else whom we're fortunate enough to call friends. You've inspired us, with your stories, your presence, your perseverance, and your support, and though we constantly ask why you stick around, we'll take it. A special thanks to Shirin, whose wisdom guided us all. And, also, thank you to every Uber driver who had to listen to us go on and on about ourselves, whilst singing along to Taylor/Britney/Mariah, and having no shame.

About My Therapist Says

My Therapist Says is the brainchild of us, four best friends and sisters—Lola Tash, Nicole Argiris, Gina Tash, and Nora Tash—who needed an outlet for both our anxiety and ridiculous stories, which we felt would be better chronicled anonymously on Instagram, with the humor our friends have come to expect from us.

Within a year, our Instagram account became a viral sensation and grew into a business of its own. Our "biting sarcasm," "keen sense of humor," and general delusion has garnered 5+ million followers, a marketing company, and a mental health initiative.

With a goal of destigmatizing mental health, and finding the humor in the mistakes our mental health journeys have led us on, the next outlets for us are a podcast to talk shit and a TV show loosely based on the inception of our brand.